W9-BTD-777

HOW STUDENTS REALLY LEARN

INSTRUCTIONAL STRATEGIES THAT WORK

LINDA HENSHALL WILSON

Rowman & Littlefield Education
Lanham, Maryland • Toronto • Oxford
2006

Published in the United States of America
by Rowman & Littlefield Education
A Division of Rowman & Littlefield Publishers, Inc.
A wholly owned subsidary of The Rowman & Littlefield Publishing Group,
Inc.
4501 Forbes Boulevard, Suite 200, Lanham, Maryland 20706
www.rowmaneducation.com

PO Box 317
Oxford
OX2 9RU, UK

British Library Cataloguing in Publication Information Available

Library of Congress Cataloging-in-Publication Data

Wilson, Linda Henshall, 1952-
  How students really learn : instructional strategies that work / Linda
Henshall Wilson.
     p. cm.
  Includes bibliographical references.
  ISBN-13: 978-1-57886-277-1 (hardcover : alk. paper)
  ISBN-10: 1-57886-277-9 (hardcover : alk. paper)
  ISBN-13: 978-1-57886-495-9 (pbk. : alk. paper)
  ISBN-10: 1-57886-495-X (pbk. : alk. paper)
  1. Learning. 2. Educational psychology. 3. Cognitive styles. 4. Early
childhood education—Methodology. I. Title.
  LB1060.W555 2006
  370.15'23—dc22   2006007585

∞™ The paper used in this publication meets the minimum requirements of
American National Standard for Information Sciences—Permanence of Paper
for Printed Library Materials, ANSI/NISO Z39.48-1992.
Manufactured in the United States of America.

To those who share my passion and love
of teaching. May your journey be filled
with shining moments each day. Teach as if
you were teaching your children or grandchildren.
You may have mine one day.

A special thank you to my teachers—at church,
public school, and the higher education level.
Special honor goes to my first teachers—my parents
and sister. Thank you to my husband, Allan,
for encouragement and support during the
writing process as well as every day.
Love to my students, past, present, and future,
especially my son, Scott, and my granddaughter,
Hailey. Thank you for rekindling my joy for
teaching each day.

CONTENTS

INTRODUCTION

This book is designed for elementary teacher education candidates, elementary teachers, parents helping their children at
home with school work, homeschool parents, principals, superintendents, members of the board of education, individuals who volunteer their time to work with elementary-aged students, and individuals who provide religious training to children—in a nutshell this
book is intended for those devoting their personal and professional
time to working with children who wish to improve their teaching so
their students will improve learning.

My first book, *Teaching 201: Traveling Beyond the Basics*, focused
on the topic of teaching. This book takes on the ultimate goal of any
teacher, *student learning*! Teachers now have a super power-charged
goal that needs an exponent added to it—*long-term learning* or *learning*^{2}. It is learning to a higher power, in mathematical terms. Rather
than being able to regurgitate a one-word answer at the end of a lesson, long-term learning means that the student has stored this information in a file folder in the brain, through assimilation and ac-
commodation, and he or she can retrieve it over and over again. The
information is *learned*.

As a university professor, I have been fascinated with recent
books on brain research. The contents contain simple suggestions
that lead to long-term learning. This book promotes simple changes
to your daily interaction with students that are free or inexpensive

and also align with the most recent brain research. These changes can provide the students with an enriched learning environment.

This book has a large intended readership. Who should buy and utilize this book? Classroom teachers in the field, preservice teachers or teacher education candidates, alternative certification teachers, homeschool parents, community volunteers who work with children, religious teachers who work with children on a weekly basis or after-school basis, administrators, and parents who wish to help their children after school, on weekends, or during the summer learn to the best of their abilities. Each chapter offers a summary for each group. Throughout the chapters, information and suggestions are made for each group. I have been a community volunteer helping with the story hour at the public library. I have taught Bible school and Sunday school. I have worked with my son to help him after school and on weekends. I have taught students (elementary, secondary, and adult learners) since 1975. I have worked with teacher education candidates since 1998 and know what content they need to go out into the classrooms. Among my students in over thirty different university courses have been alternative certification teachers. I have a doctorate degree in educational leadership, formerly referred to as educational administration. I am certified as an elementary principal and also as a superintendent of schools. I understand the vital role of the administrator in helping the faculty create learning opportunities that will produce long-term learning for students. I've been in the shoes of the intended readership. I believe that this information will be beneficial and vital to each of you.

- Classroom teachers, preservice teachers or teacher education candidates, alternative certification teachers, administrators: Each group will have similar requirements whether you work at a public or private school. Employ the suggestions and recommendations from this book to best benefit your students. Administrators will read from a "teacher's point of view" and be able to best lead your faculty into the twenty-first century of teaching and learning. When faculty members want to begin new things in their enriched learning environment, you will know the brain research background for their requests.

- Community volunteers and religious teachers: This book will provide you with the most current teaching techniques that will help you to create and maintain an enriched learning environment for your students.

- Homeschool parents: This book will address the best and most recent brain research information that you can directly apply to your enriched learning environment. Whether you have taken training seminars or not, you will be best prepared to work with your children after reading this book.

- Parents: You will be able to read the information for the other groups and select the best activities for your children. You will be prepared for the comment from your child, "I'm bored!" He or she will not be bored when you pull out the bag of tricks you have learned from the contents of this book. Chapters 14, 15, and 16 will be especially helpful to you. You and your child can make the projects together. They require household items that are readily available in your home.

The learner has changed dramatically over the past few decades. Teachers today have a multitude of "extras" at their disposal to help students learn the content. Yet many teachers are still using the same rote teaching styles that were used fifty years ago. We are not teaching the same type of students. These children will grow up with technology all around them. These students have unlimited opportunities for jobs in fields yet to be discovered. Children are still asked, however, to complete worksheets as students did decades ago. There just *has* to be a better way—and there is! There are better ways to teach so that students will learn—long-term learning, learning to a higher power, learning^2—rather than a one-word regurgitation on a worksheet. Read the contents of this book to find out.

Educators know that students learn in one of three learning styles. According to Madeline Hunter, "Expecting all children the same age to learn from the same materials is like expecting all children the same age to wear the same size clothing" (*Hoagie's Gifted Education*,

2006).Today the various learning styles can be transformed into statistics and broken down into 46 percent visual learners, 35 percent kinesthetic learners, and 19 percent auditory learners.

This ratio does not appeal to the "read and fill in the blank" type of teaching that is still being used in classrooms today. The suggestions for lessons in this book include ideas that appeal to at least two and most often all three learning styles. Because there are so many visual learners—almost one half of all learners are visual—suggestions such as adding color or various textures will help those learners make it to learning[2] When you add the visual and kinesthetic learner numbers, we find that 81 percent of our students learn in this manner. Remembering these facts about the students within our classrooms, revisit the methods used in today's classrooms. We do not have "fill in the blank" students. We have *touch* and *see* and *do* and *create* learners today. They do not want to fill in the blanks. They want to discover the answers to divergent questions. To quote Roger Lewin (as cited in *Hoagie's Gifted Education*, 2006), "Too often we give children answers to remember rather than problems to solve."

I invite you to pick and choose any of the suggestions to use in your classroom or home study environment. Add your personal touches to these ideas to best assist the child learn, retain knowledge, and—most importantly—love learning! Happy reading, happy teaching, and happy learning! Your journey begins.

REFERENCE

Hoagie's gifted education: Education quotes. (2006). Retrieved from www .hoagiesgifted.org/education_quotes.htm.

I

LEARNING, A TO Z

1

HOW WE LEARN

The important thing is not so much that every child should be taught, as that every child should be given the wish to learn.

—John Lubbock

Every student can learn, just not on the same day, or the same way.

—George Evans

Expecting all children the same age to learn from the same materials is like expecting all children the same age to wear the same size clothing.

—Madeline Hunter

This chapter offers a review of learning styles for the teachers and administrators. The information will be new to the teacher education candidates, parents, community volunteers, and religious teachers reading this book. All readers will enjoy learning about the "fourth learning modality." A web address is provided for the readers to take the VARK inventory and discover their own learning modality.

CHAPTER 1

THE "BIG THREE" LEARNING STYLES

Educators have grouped the way we learn into three basic areas referred to as learning styles. We are auditory, kinesthetic, or visual
learners. Auditory learners hear or listen and process that information.
Listening tapes, class or group discussions, and short teacher lectures
are wonderful for these students. Kinesthetic learners learn by doing.
Math manipulatives, science experiments, and activities considered
hands-on are tailored to kinesthetic learners. The visual learners see
the information and retain it. Visual learners benefit from the use of
overhead transparencies, interactive bulletin boards, and various instructional charts. The addition of color is very beneficial to visual
learners. The classroom teacher can organize the day's agenda on a
whiteboard using a different color for morning and afternoon or a different color for each subject to appeal to the visual learner. According
to Sousa (1998), the average classroom has 46 percent visual learners,
35 percent kinesthetic learners, and 19 percent auditory learners.

When examining the "46-35-19" breakdown of learning styles
within a classroom more closely, almost one half of all the learners
are visual learners. How will you arrange your classroom, decorate
your classroom, and use color in your lessons to help these students
learn, retain knowledge, and love learning? Those questions are answered within the pages of this book. Just over one third of all learners are kinesthetic learners. Again, what will you do when designing
lessons and activities to best help these students learn by doing?
This book gives you a wealth of avenues to assist these students.

Consider the three learning styles when designing learning opportunities for your students. Provide assignments that appeal to
more than one of the above-mentioned learning modalities. Try, if
possible, to utilize all three modalities in your learning opportunities. I refer to this as a "home run"—all the bases are touched.

THE FOURTH LEARNING STYLE

A fourth learning style has emerged—the reading/writing group.
This is a unique modality. It is not seen in primary students who are

still emergent readers and writers. This modality comes into its own as the student develops and perfects these skills. It can be assumed that we see the reading/writing learners at the middle school, high school, and adult learner levels.

Before attempting to understand the learning modalities of a classroom or group of children, why not find out *your* modality? Each semester I require my elementary methods students (my future teachers) to take the VARK inventory. This is the favorite assignment for the entire semester—every semester. The assignment promotes much reflection and analysis of results.

Teacher, Know Thyself

As teachers or adults planning learning opportunities for children, we often fall into a comfort zone when designing lessons. We teach *our* learning modality—it is the easiest for us. Think back to your favorite teachers in school. Most likely, they taught to your learning modality.

Knowing your modality can help you teach outside your teaching comfort zone, providing learning opportunities for *every* child. Log on to the following website to learn *your* modality: www.vark-learn.com or www.vark-learn.com/english/index.asp (Fleming, 2006). This is the site for the VARK inventory. You will learn your primary and also secondary modalities. It is interesting to know both the strongest and second or secondary modality. Going back to Sousa's statistics once again, if 46 percent of all learners are considered visual learners, what would the results be if we included the second modality results in that data? If more than one third of all learners in the classroom are considered kinesthetic learners, how would that figure change when you add in the second modality? When designing learning opportunities for students, you are appealing to both the dominant learning modality and also the second modality.

I have taken the test a few times and the results always come back the same. When reflecting on the results, I can easily see why I preferred specific learning opportunities over others. Most importantly, I can see why I teach the way I do—or *did* before I took into account my students' needs.

After learning your modality, you now know your teaching comfort zone. Teach outside that zone. Challenge yourself to design innovative ways in which your students can learn using all the learning modalities. You will enjoy getting out of the teaching rut, and your students will benefit from their new learning opportunities.

Applying the Learning Styles

The best example of using all three learning modalities to best help students learn is the weekly spelling lessons. Every teacher on the planet assesses the students with a weekly spelling test, generally given on Friday. The students *hear* the word and *write* it down. But *how* does the student learn to spell? Creative and innovative classroom teachers will take the three learning modalities into consideration when planning learning opportunities for their students. (Chapter 14 provides many creative and innovative examples to help children spell using the learning styles.)

Classroom teachers who consider classroom discipline and management will think these activities through and establish guidelines or rules *prior* to sharing them with the students. Use common sense and forethought with these activities. Consider setting class guidelines or rules for group learning prior to a group learning activity. You know the atmosphere you wish to create and maintain in your classroom. Take the initiative to establish and maintain it prior to the activities. (Chapter 11 provides steps to help you set guidelines for the enriched learning environment.)

Auditory

Auditory learners would benefit from *hearing* the list of spelling words spelled correctly. This could be achieved by creating a listening center where the students could spend time listening to an auditory tape specially created with the spelling words. This could also be achieved by playing the tape in the mornings as the students arrive in class. Using downtime wisely will benefit your students. The tape could be played as the students prepare to go to lunch or get ready to leave at the end of the day. The teacher can create the tape, or this could be a group, individual, or class project. Also consider playing soft music in the background to break the monotony.

Parents can work with their children to create an auditory tape to listen to at home. Do you transport your child to school? Use that driving time in the car to multitask by listening to an auditory tape of the week's spelling words. Play the tape in the mornings at home as your child is getting ready for the day. Involve your child in the determination of the best time to play the listening tape.

Suggestion: Do not destroy the tape after the spelling test has been completed. Continue to add to it. The full tape will be an excellent source of review for the students, especially during the weekends, holidays, or over the summer vacation.

Visual and Kinesthetic

The visual and kinesthetic modalities can be combined for opportunities to learn spelling. Children love to write with colored pencils or markers. The use of colors when writing the words will help the visual learner and also involve the kinesthetic learner during the actual writing process. Identifying specific parts of the word will help the visual learners. For example, writing the prefix or suffix in a different color will help the student *see* the root word with the colored addition. Again, as the student physically writes the word, the kinesthetic modality is enhanced.

Do you have a plastic placemat at home? Classroom teachers can use the student desks for the next learning opportunity. The adult sprays a small amount of shaving cream onto the specific area. The students are asked to spread out the cream into a thin layer. As the adult says the spelling word, the students "write" the word with an index finger in the cream. The student can then self-check the word for accuracy. A quick move of the hand and the student is ready to spell another word. This activity can be done with a small group, an entire classroom, or a single student. An advantage to this activity is a clean work space when the students finish. Be sure to have paper towels on hand to wipe the desks clean when the project is completed. Parents using a placemat at home can easily rinse it off in the kitchen sink. This activity can also be completed using a colored plastic plate. The white shaving cream works in contrast to the colored background. Avoid using a white plate with white shaving cream. There is no contrast for the student to see.

I have used the above activity with adult learners. It seems that students of all ages love to write in shaving cream. As the classroom teacher, I modeled the activity for the students. They all relished seeing their professor roll up her sleeves and get her hands creamy. Because this was a social studies methods course, we could use the round plate to represent the world and draw in the major lines of latitude. We could also draw the hemispheres or continents or, thinking more locally, draw one state. We were also able to recycle the plates for future semesters.

Building on the shaving cream activity, use sugar or salt sprinkled on the plate instead of shaving cream. This is less messy and possibly less expensive. Sugar or salt is also readily available in most households as opposed to shaving cream. You can reuse the plastic plates for another spelling lesson. You can also store the sugar or salt in a resealable plastic bag for future use. Your initial cost will seem small if you spread it over the school year. Just as with the shaving cream, please use *colored* plastic plates when using sugar or salt to have a contrast for the student to see.

If the students can write using cursive, consider asking them to "write" their spelling words using string or yarn. These items can be part of your wish list at the beginning of the school year. As with sugar and salt, most households have bits and pieces of twine, string, or colored yarn available. Ask the student to write the spelling word using a pencil, pen, or colored marker. Then ask them to trace the word using string, twine, or yarn. They can snip small pieces to dot i's or cross t's or x's. If time allows, they can glue down the yarn or string. After the glue is dried, they can do a rubbing by using plain white paper (photocopy paper works well) and a crayon. The rubbing will show the spelling word in any color you choose.

Another great activity is to incorporate puzzles into the weekly spelling lesson. You can type the spelling words using different fonts and font sizes. Cut the words out and glue them down onto a sheet of photocopy paper at different angles on the page. Duplicate enough sheets for your entire class. Use a paper cutter to cut each sheet into a puzzle. Put the pieces into a resealable sandwich-sized bag, or use a paperclip to hold the puzzle together. Continue the process until you have enough puzzles for each student. Older students can use colored markers to create a puzzle for another student in the classroom. They also learn as they write the words. Parents can hand write the words around the page and then cut it up into a puzzle for their child. I taught fifth grade for many years. We were often asked to help with a project for the kindergarten or first grade classes. We used inside recess time during bad weather to complete these projects. Primary teachers can involve older students with this learning opportunity.

A fun addition to the puzzle idea is to add a quote to the page. Perhaps your school has a motto or a school song. You could write that on the page. Let those creative juices flow to add a special message within the puzzle.

Alphabet macaroni and cereal can be used to spell words. The students select the correct letters and physically manipulate the macaroni to form the desired word correctly. Again be aware of the addition of color. If the students' desks are dark, macaroni will show up well. If the desks are light in color, consider giving each student a sheet of black or brown construction paper as a background. This will help contrast the macaroni and enhance the visual learning experience for the student. Use a contrasting background when using alphabet-shaped cereal with the students as well.

Have a game plan ready for distributing and collecting the macaroni or cereal. It would be easiest for the teacher to put a handful inside a resealable bag for each student prior to the activity. Student helpers can assist in passing out and picking up the manipulatives. If the cereal is to be used as a snack, a classroom helper (or the helper of the day or the week) can pass out coffee filters. The teacher can use latex gloves to put the cereal into each coffee filter. The filters are very cost-effective.

Apply to Other Curricular Areas

The spelling activities for the auditory, visual, and kinesthetic learners can be transposed into other subject areas as well. Vocabulary terms in reading, science, and social studies can be creatively used with a tape recorder or transformed into a puzzle. The shaving cream, salt, and sugar activity can be used with young children learning to write their numbers and letters. It can also be used as a fun activity with mathematics problems. These core activities can help students learn the objective and subjective pronouns, tenses of verbs, and even words and phrases in foreign languages.

When designing these activities for your students, have your ducks in a row prior to the learning opportunity. For example, set ground rules in advance to avoid having shaving cream all over the classroom. The students cannot bite off pieces of the cereal or macaroni to create a new letter. An R cannot be changed to a P. (Yes, I *have* done these activities with my students!) If the macaroni and cereal are to be reused several times, they are not a snack item.

Consider the abilities of your students. The activities can be independent or completed by a small group. If you have a group activity, again you must discuss guidelines with the students prior to the activity. Some teachers have classroom rules posted in their classrooms just for group activities.

We have taken the mundane task of learning the week's spelling words and transformed the task into creative and innovative ways in which students can use their learning modalities. This can be done individually or in a small group. Parents working with their children at home or classroom teachers can prepare in advance to have supplies ready and guidelines established prior to the activity. If you can make spelling fun and exciting, what can you do with math facts or science terms? The sky is the limit!

MULTIPLE INTELLIGENCES

No chapter on how we learn could be complete without including information on multiple intelligences. This first came to the forefront when Howard Gardner wrote *Frames of Mind: The Theory of Multiple Intelligences* in 1983. Up until that time, teachers had always suspected that students had a major strength area, but it was only a suspicion. Gardner identified eight target areas in which children—and adults—have special interests, abilities, talents, gifts, or intelligences.

I always tell my adult learners that grandparents love Howard Gardner! Every grandparent on the planet (including me) just happens to have a grandchild that is special. They draw better than any other child. Or perhaps they are the best gymnast in their group. Grandparents rarely see the flaws in children; they only see the "intelligences." That's where Gardner and grandparents see the world through the same eyes. In an educational system that labels children as LD, MR, ED, ADD, ADHD, and OCD, to mention just a few, Gardner takes a look at a child and asks, "How are you gifted?" Grandparents just love this guy! How would our educational system change if we all took the approach that Gardner takes with children or learners?

A summary of Gardner's seven intelligences (1983) follows:

1. Interpersonal intelligence: has a high level of ability to understand the feelings, desires, and ideas of others.
2. Intrapersonal intelligence: is highly aware of one's self and introspective. Self-motivated and independent worker.
3. Verbal/linguistic intelligence: has a high-level use of language—writing, reading, and speaking.
4. Spatial intelligence: has a high ability to organize the world through spatial relations. Interacts with the world through seeing, hearing, tasting, touching, and smelling.
5. Logical/mathematical intelligence: uses both inductive and deductive reasoning skills and views the world through a mathematical perspective. Has a high ability to classify, illustrate relationships, and recognize patterns. Transfers numbers, symbols, and concepts of mathematics to other curricular areas and the world.
6. Bodily/kinesthetic intelligence: learns best through movement activities. Excels in sports, dance, and other movement activities.

7. Musical intelligence: has a high sensitivity to rhythm, pitch, key, melody, harmony, chords, and timbre. Has the ability to use the components of music to play and also create new musical forms and compositions.

Gardner has not completed his work on multiple intelligences. He is still examining other areas to see if they meet the criteria as an *intelligence*. More recently Gardner has looked at the area of naturalistic intelligence, which shows a high sense of the interconnectedness and relationships of the elements of nature. Other areas Gardner is examining are spiritual, existential, and moral intelligences.

Teacher, Know Thyself

Just as you need to know your specific learning style, you also need to know your intelligence. Be prepared to have strong first intelligence and a close second one. If you have children, perhaps they have the same strengths that you have. Did they inherit them, or did you enhance them through repetition and example? My son is super in spatial intelligence or spatial awareness. Yes, that is a strong area for me also. This helps him as a flight instructor and pilot—especially while flying at night.

My future teachers/university students all take the VARK inventory as well as a multiple intelligence quiz to find out their strengths and weak areas. You can find numerous MI quizzes on the Internet. Most often, the students agree with the test results. They then start to "analyze" their roommate or their spouse or their parents. As teachers, we will start to analyze our students. It is to our advantage to know their learning styles and multiple intelligence strength area.

Throughout the chapters of this book, you will read about activities for children that appeal to the various learning styles—and multiple intelligences. By designing lessons that enhance your students' multiple intelligences, you will also be designing lessons that include the elements of the three learning modalities. What a wonderful experience for your students! What a wonderful way to promote long-term learning or learning[2].

- Summary for administrators: Emphasize the importance of creating learning opportunities for children that utilize the three learning styles. Provide a way for your teachers to find out their own learning style and multiple intelligence. You find out which way you learn best also. Take the quizzes. Involved leaders encourage their followers. Work at the district level to offer professional development opportunities for your faculty in this area. The children will benefit greatly from this way of teaching. Long-term learning or learning^2 will occur within the walls of your school site.

  Encourage your teachers to provide creative and innovative learning opportunities for children. Provide a way for teachers to share their innovative lessons with others at your site or in your district.

  Invite the local newspaper editor to visit with teachers for possible articles about these lessons. Invite the local or area television station to feature a human interest story about one of your creative teachers. Take pride in being the leader of an out-of-the-box teaching and learning school site. Word of caution: Work within the district policy for photos of students published in the newspaper or shown on television. You may need parent release forms signed, and so on.

  Work with new teachers to provide time for them to visit creative classrooms to get ideas. Assign one of the innovative teachers to mentor a new teacher at your site.

  Schedule grade level meeting times to share innovative teaching strategies that lead to long-term learning.

  Reward the out-of-the-box teachers with the opportunity to work with teacher education candidates. Best practices need to be passed along to future teachers.

  As the leader of curriculum at your school site, offer mini-workshops on the writings and works of the various educational theorists. It may have been many years since some of your teachers studied this. Most alternative certification teachers have never studied the educational masters. Provide ways for your faculty to revisit or visit for the first time the theories of Jean Piaget, David Ausubel, Jerome Bruner, Lev Vygotsky, and Howard Gardner.

- Summary for teachers: Make changes for the dull and boring "writing the spelling words x number of times" assignment each Monday. Try a suggestion from chapter 1 each week. Provide variety for your students. Tell them on Friday about the new lesson you have in store for them on Monday. They will be excited about coming to your classroom on Monday. They will tell their family about the wonderful learning opportunities they have at school. Their motivation and enthusiasm will become contagious in your classroom.

   Share your creative teaching ideas with other teachers. Submit an idea to a national teaching magazine so professionals across the nation will benefit from you.

   Work with your administrator to bring in future teachers (teacher education candidates) to observe innovative teaching practices. These students will benefit from their observations— and share the ideas with their peers and professors.

- Summary for community volunteers and religious teachers: You may be working with your group of children for an hour per week. What suggestions from this chapter can you employ for your group? How can you modify the puzzle example or the shaving cream example to work with your students? What information could you put on an audio cassette tape for them to review over the week? Read this chapter again. Use one of these ideas next week with your students.

- Summary for homeschool parents: The suggestions from this chapter utilize readily available materials that you have in your home today. Select the ideas that will work best with your child.

   Give your children two or three options from the suggestions in this chapter. Ask them to select which one they want to use this week. Their choice will probably be a signal to you about which one is their strongest learning style.

REFERENCES

Fleming, N. (2006). *VARK—A guide to learning styles.* Retrieved from www
.vark-learn.com.

Gardner, H. (1983). *Frames of Mind: The theory of multiple intelligences.* New
York: Basic Books.

Sousa, D. (1998). *How the brain learns: More new insights for educators.*
A presentation on August 18, 1998, Port Washington, WI.

2

WHEN DO WE LEARN?

It is the supreme art of the teacher to awaken joy in creative expression and knowledge.

—Albert Einstein

The question of "when?" is a huge question to tackle regarding student learning. Too often the choice of opportune times to teach specific items is out of the control of the classroom teacher, community leader, or religious volunteer. This chapter provides significant information for those in the out-of-control category.

We can examine the question of when student learning is at its lowest point by taking a look at the circadian rhythms or cycles of humans. Generally speaking for all age groups, "half way between the time you usually wake and the time you usually go to sleep is your low point in terms of energy and alertness" (Howard, 2000).

Transposing Howard's midpoint downtime cycle into our daily lives and the lives of our students is interesting. Take a look from the classroom teacher's point of view. An elementary student who wakes at 7:00 A.M. and goes to sleep at 9:00 P.M. has a downtime at 2:00 P.M. This is the time of day that the student wants to curl up and snooze rather than solve higher level thinking problems. This halfway point changes for each student and especially for each age group.

ADULTS

Adult learners are divided into "larks" or "owls"—morning or evening people. Obviously, adults know into which category they fall, and they know which time of day they best learn. A recent study involving 410 participants showed that this preference for early morning or late evening is actually connected to our DNA. The participants were given a questionnaire called Horne-Ostberg, named after the two developers.

> Blood samples provided DNA that showed the existence of genes in the same location that occur in more than one form. It was found that carriers of one genotype had lower Horne-Ostberg scores, indicating an increased preference for eveningness, while the other genotype scored significantly higher than the other group, indicating increased preference for morningness. This study showed for the first time that there is a genetic component for morningness and eveningness. (*Are You an "Owl" or a "Lark"?* 1999)

According to one of the study's authors, Dr. Emmanuel Mignot, the study refers to circadian rhythms, or a person's internal clock. This internal clock controls behaviors like sleeping and waking and is tied to the 24-hour daily dark-light cycle (*Early to Bed, Early to Rise*, 1998). Scientists believe that the human circadian rhythm or cycle changes with age. Infants and senior citizens both are often awake during part of the nighttime when the rest of the world is asleep. Humans actually require different amounts of sleep as we progress through life.

MIDDLE SCHOOL AND HIGH SCHOOL STUDENTS

A frequent topic among many recent educational publications is the circadian cycle of teenagers. According to *Wikipedia*, the term "circadian" comes from the Latin *circa*, "around," and *dies*, "day," meaning literally "around a day." All organisms have circadian cycles. Some organisms have unusual circadian cycles. Some organisms are nocturnal—their circadian cycles are different from that of humans. I have often joked that teenagers are nocturnal. They are not truly nocturnal, but there is evidence that the teenage biological clock or circadian cycle is different from that of adults and also different from that of elementary students.

To help teenagers adapt best to learning, some districts are starting at the same time each day, but trying a "looping" schedule. The first day of school, the first period would be at the beginning of school. The second day of school, the second period would be at the beginning of school; the first period would be at the end of the day. The loop would continue with a different period beginning each morning. Teachers who see students asleep with their eyes open at 7:30 A.M. are able to see completely different students at 1:00 P.M.

Many districts are changing their start times to accommodate adolescents' circadian cycles. "In Minnesota, the state medical association took a stand, and wrote school superintendents a letter warning that early start times were incompatible with teenager's body clocks, and bad for health, school performance, and driving" ("Waking up to truth," 2002, p. E3).

Aside from this issue of sleep interfering with learning early each morning, "Lack of sleep also increases teenage drivers' already elevated risk of car accidents. According to the National Sleep Foundation, a nonprofit group, drowsiness or fatigue play a role in 100,000 traffic crashes a year, and drivers 25 or under cause more than half of those accidents" ("Waking up to truth," 2002, p. E3).

Many districts that changed to later start times for middle and high school students conducted follow-up studies with various groups after the first year. They had high approval ratings from parents, students, faculty, staff, and administrators. Grades improved, student alertness and participation improved (which helped to improve grades), and there were fewer discipline problems before school.

ELEMENTARY STUDENTS

We've examined the larks and owls. We've taken a look at the circadian cycle or rhythm of teenagers. It's now time to examine elementary students. The time that school starts is set by the district. Some elementary students will be starting earlier if their high school and middle school students begin later in the morning. This is a simple flip-flop process due to the limited number of school buses within the transportation system.

I often visit elementary schools, and I am amazed at the morning opening events. I understand that the teacher has to take attendance, take the lunch count, and perform various other administrative duties. The teacher almost always tells the students to "write in their journals" while they take care of these matters. I understand bell work (work that the students do when they arrive and that will soon be reviewed or discussed) that is connected to the curriculum, but teachers don't grade journals. The students receive no grade for this time frame. (This might be perceived as busy work.) There has to be a "better mousetrap" to open the day.

I would love for the teacher, community volunteer, or religious teacher to start off with a 1- to 2-minute overview of the day's agenda (which will be color-coded on the whiteboard). Begin with a "clapping time." The teacher claps a sequence and the students mimic. Welcome them, thank them for coming in quietly, and then set the stage for the remainder of the day. Make it exciting so that they can't wait to investigate new ways to add and subtract money. Have them so pumped up that they cannot wait till 11:00 when it's time to identify nouns from a newspaper story (using colored markers, of course). Get them in the palm of your hand, get their attention, and keep it for the remainder of the day. As mentioned in chapter 9, use music as a cue to begin the day. This could be before your opening few minutes or after—whichever you choose. Suggestions of songs are made in chapter 9. One suggestion is "We Will Rock You." That song involves clapping, and you could add stomping as well. It would get them moving, listening, and ready for the day.

Step back and examine the previous paragraph. We are appealing to the visual, kinesthetic, and auditory learners. We're using color for the visual students, music and verbal explanations for the auditory students, and clapping and stomping—movement—for the kinesthetic students. (Note: If you feel that the clapping and stomping would be too noisy for other classrooms, consider "air clapping" in which the students clap but their hands do not touch; thus, no noise. The same can be done with "air stomping," or the students can move only their big toe, which will also be silent. Try this out to "We Will Rock You"—it works!) This morning scenario appeals to all learning styles—and we just used it to get their attention for a minute or two.

Now that we have the students' attention and are ready for the learning process to begin, it would be wonderful for teachers to use the entire morning for the core curriculum areas. Remember Howard's example at the beginning of the chapter about the midway point in our days? Elementary students will experience downtime in early afternoon. It would be great to use the remainder of the day for other academics as well as visits to the library, computer lab, music room, gymnasium, and other ports of call. Unfortunately the library, computer lab, and the other destinations would be empty during the mornings and jam-packed during the afternoons. We have to construct a schedule that fits with all the other teachers in our building. We also have to accommodate all special services students who might be pulled out throughout the day. Our schedule revolves around that of the resource lab, speech lab, physical therapy lab, remedial reading resource room, mathematics resource room, and any other possible pullout that may be available to the students. Juggling to create a feasible schedule for all students can be exhausting. Erlauer (2003) suggests rotating instruction daily to avoid teaching the same subject during downtime each day. If at all possible, this would be a great solution for many elementary students and teachers.

We have few choices about when we can teach specific subjects, but how can we use our time frame for the lessons to be most advantageous?

A. The 10 minute rule: Consider when students are best prepared for learning within the lesson time frame. According to Sousa (1998), the first 10 minutes of a lesson is the time when students will learn the most. This is paramount for teachers, homeschool teachers, community volunteers, and religious teachers. Get in as much as possible within the first 10 minutes.

B. The 20 minute rule: Attention span studies of children and young adults show that students need a break in concentration at least every 20 minutes, according to Sousa (1995). Again, this is a paramount concept for teachers, community volunteers, religious teachers, and homeschool teachers to consider when preparing to work with students in this age group. Have you ever sat in a meeting and had your mind wander off to what you will be cooking for dinner or which items you needed to pick up at the store? This open-eyed yet detached from the conversation behavior is the same way students react in the classroom after sitting and listening for over 20 minutes. They may go a step further and begin to write notes or need to sharpen a pencil—they begin kinesthetic activities along with their mental detachment from the topic. Politely stated: you've lost them! You sound like the teacher in the Charlie Brown cartoons. Keeping the 20 minute rule in mind, design lessons that are short on teacher lecture and long on visual and kinesthetic activities. Make every effort possible to keep them actively engaged in the learning process. They can be constructing, discussing, comparing and contrasting, manipulating materials, pasting or gluing—anything but sitting and listening after the 20-minute time frame. Returning again to the concept of read the narrative or set of pages or section and answer the questions. This does not promote active engagement in the learning process. (But it is a great way to have a quiet classroom for a few minutes!)

Going back to Part A: Design a powerful, action- and fact-packed first 10 minutes.

Learning from Part B: Limit sitting and listening to only 20 minutes.

C. Spend the first two or three sentences of the lesson with a quick verbal review. "As you recall, yesterday we learned about the earth's crust. Today we are going to learn about a place beneath the crust called the mantle." In two sentences you have brought them up to speed and set the stage for today's lesson. Your next sentence would be your introduction to the lesson. This is considered good practice among educators. It also coincides with the writings and teachings of Jean Piaget. I used to teach multiple reading lessons and math lessons each day when I taught third grade. I couldn't remember what we did yesterday without referring to my lesson plan. Sometimes I would ask the students to tell the group what we learned yesterday in mathematics. "Susan, would you please tell the group what we did yesterday in math class?" Susan would give a one-sentence response, I would thank her, and I would tell them what we would be doing today. We were all on the same page. We would then proceed to the introduction and get the learning process into full gear.

Going back to Part A: Design a powerful, action- and fact-packed first 10 minutes.

Learning from Part B: Limit sitting and listening to only 20 minutes.

Applying Part C: Give a brief review from yesterday before proceeding with today's topic.

D. Have visuals, manipulatives, and any other necessary items ready to go. Remember, most learning takes place within the first 10 minutes of the lesson. Don't waste time being unprepared. I used to adjust the focus on the overhead projector to be sure it was set prior to class time. Having the manipulatives counted and ready in resealable bags or placed in coffee filters is a huge time saver for teachers. (Coffee filters are very cost-effective and are great holders for small items such as magnets, alphabet macaroni, plastic letters, puzzle pieces, etc.) If the students need supplies such as crayons, rulers, or scissors, please tell them in advance to get these items out. I often see lessons in which the teacher is finished with instruction and the students didn't know what supplies they need. Communicate this information well—write it on the whiteboard or chalkboard for them in advance. If the students are to use the classroom computers for a writing assignment, be sure they have their floppy, CD, or flashdrive ready to copy their work. Preparation before the lesson will help prevent any disturbance or interruption of the learning process.

Going back to Part A: Design a powerful, action- and fact-packed first 10 minutes.

Learning from Part B: Limit sitting and listening to only 20 minutes.

Reviewing Part C: Give a brief review from yesterday before proceeding with today's topic.

Applying Part D: Make every effort to be prepared. Use the information from the previous pages to incorporate the use of color, music, and other brain friendly strategies into your lessons.

E. Give the students a purpose. Teachers are continually asking the students to "read the story or text and answer the questions." If you go over the questions first, the students will have a purpose for reading the story. This gives the students an opportunity to ask questions if they don't understand a term within the question. This is also a great test-taking skill—have them look over the options on a multiple-choice test before reading the question stem.

Going back to Part A: Design a powerful, action- and fact-packed first 10 minutes.

Learning from Part B: Limit sitting and listening to only 20 minutes.

Reviewing Part C: Give a brief review from yesterday before proceeding with today's topic.

Revisiting Part D: Make every effort to be prepared. Use the information from the previous pages to incorporate the use of color, music, and other brain friendly strategies into your lessons.

Applying Part E: Give them a purpose for the lesson prior to making assignments.

F. Most importantly, during the lesson, make every effort to make the topic *relevant* to the students. If they connect, they'll want to learn it, and, most importantly, they'll retain it. They will assimilate and accommodate and store it as long-term learning or learning[2]. Find ways to make connections to some part of their daily lives or something that they are knowledgeable about. Students who are poor math students always come to life when the topic of money is introduced into the lesson. Adding, subtracting, multiplying, and dividing with decimals is not that far from completing the same processes with money— use both the 10ths and 100ths place. Bring in plastic money for them to use as manipulatives. Ask them to design a $1,000,000 bill and write a two-paragraph rationale to support their choice. The topic of money leads to the study of the history of money. When did America first print paper money? When did America first make coin money? What material or metal was used? Compare the recent evolution of paper money—they now have incorporated different colors. You could teach forever on the historical backgrounds of the state quarters or the Westward Journey Series (see the U.S. Mint website at www.usmint.gov). These are examples of relevance in teaching that promotes learning. Do some "couch mining," or go through your pockets to find great learning manipulatives for your students.

Often the students will ask, "Why do we have to do this?" The logical answer is, "Because I am the teacher!" A more creative response might be, "Because I love to grade papers." When students feel that the assignment is busy work, the topic or assignment has no relevance for them. Make every effort during the lesson to make the topic connect with the students. Help them to see the relevance of the lesson and how it connects to the *previous* lesson or how it will connect to the *next* lesson. In conclusion, relevance is huge when coupled with learning. Keep this in mind throughout your lessons and preparation of lessons.

G. Conclusion and preview: Every lesson needs a conclusion. I always tell my university students that fishing is like teaching. You carefully select your lure or bait—that's the *planning* phase. You cast into the water—*introduction* of the lesson. The movement and wiggling of the pole—*instruction*. You catch the fish—*learning*! The ultimate goal of fishing is catching the fish; the ultimate goal of teaching is student learning—long-term learning or learning[2]. You take the fish off the hook and put it on the stringer or in the live well, or if you are a conservationist, you return it to the water to be caught another day—*conclusion*. I like to include a preview of tomorrow's lesson during this time. Just as Part C involved only two or three sentences, the conclusion and preview of tomorrow's lesson/topic also is quite short. As you *reviewed* yesterday's topic, also include a very short *preview* of tomorrow. This shows good planning on your part. It is also considered good practice, or best practice as it is referred to in educational circles.

- Summary for administrators: Examine closely the latest information regarding the circadian cycle. Share this information with other colleagues within the district.
- Provide professional development for your faculty and also parents regarding this issue.
- Summary for teachers: When planning lessons, take the sections A through G into consideration.

   Restructure your opening exercise for the day. How will you get the students' attention and keep it?
- Summary for homeschool parents: Remember the 10 minute rule and the 20 minute rule when working with your children.

   Perhaps the information about the circadian cycle will be of help to you when working with your child.

• Summary for community and religious volunteers: Take the contents of this chapter and tailor it to meet the needs of your students. Sections A through G will be helpful.

REFERENCES

Are you an "owl" or a "lark"? (1999). Retrieved April 10, 2006, from www .stanford.edu/~dement/clock.html

Early to bed, early to rise? (1998). Retrieved April 10, 2006, from www.stanford.edu/~dement/early.html.

Erlauer, L. (2003). *The brain-compatible classroom: Using what we know about learning to improve teaching.* Alexandria, VA: Association for Supervision and Curriculum Development.

Howard, P. J. (2000). *The owner's manual for the brain.* Austin, TX: Bard Press.

Sousa, D. (1995). *How the brain learns.* Reston, VA: National Association of Secondary School Principals.

Sousa, D. (1998). *How the brain learns: More new insights for educators.* A presentation on August 18, 1998, Port Washington, WI.

Waking up to truth about teens and sleep. (2002, December 1). *Minneapolis Star Tribune*, p. E3.

3

DIFFERENCES IN GENDER AND LEARNING

You can teach a student a lesson for a day; but if you can teach him to learn by creating curiosity, he will continue the learning process as long as he lives.

—Clay P. Bedford

From the past chapters you have learned how we learn and how teachers can improve learning. This chapter takes a look at the differences between boys and girls and how the teacher can use this information to create an effective learning environment for every student. Teachers and administrators will see statistics that perhaps prove what they have suspected and observed throughout their careers. Community volunteers will find this information very helpful when planning activities and learning opportunities for students of both genders. Homeschool parents will agree with much of the information if they are working with both genders.

The most recent statistics show that in classrooms across the country, about 88 to 90 percent of classroom teachers are female. This statistic is for teachers in 4-year-old programs or kindergarten through high school senior programs. The statistics for only elementary school would be even higher. Female teachers are designing and creating lessons based on their learning preferences. Female teachers are also teaching male students much more frequently than male teachers are teaching female students.

I was at an advantage as a classroom teacher because I was the mother of a son. I lived with a little boy and heard life from his perspective on a daily basis. I also heard his perspective about boring lessons on a daily basis. I still struggled daily to try to understand the boys in my classroom. At times their behaviors were unpredictable and unreasonable—from a female's point of view. I realize now that a male teacher would have understood the boys' behaviors much more easily.

BULLYING—BOYS VERSUS GIRLS

The topic of bullying is a major issue in educational circles today. Leonard Sax sheds light on this topic in *Why Gender Matters: What Parents and Teachers Need to Know About the Emerging Science of Sex Differences* (2005). Being an educator since 1975, I thought that a bully was the stereotypical boy who was stocky or chubby, wearing the beanie with the propeller on top, and antagonizing smaller or younger kids out of their lunch money or lunches.

Sax (2005) paints a much different picture. Yes, some boys can be bullies. Yes, they can wear the beanie with the propeller on top. They also have specific traits, according to Sax (2005). Male bullies have few friends. They are socially inept. Academically they do poorly in school. Male bullies don't know or know well the person they are bullying. And, a key difference between male and female bullies, they bully alone.

As a student, I never encountered the freckle-faced bully wanting my lunch or my lunch money. (Perhaps that's because I grew up across the street from school and always went home for lunch; thus, I was broke each day.) I thought I had never encountered a female bully until reading Sax's book. I *have* met them in my own life as a child and also as an adult. I can name names. According to Sax (2005), female bullies are well connected with a social circle. They are not loners like their male counterparts. They have fine-tuned social skills. Female bullies do well academically. They know the individual they are bullying well. Generally, they use key personal information as part of the bullying technique. Female bullies work in groups rather than alone to complete the bullying process.

Many states have mandated "bullying policies." A result of many of these state mandates is that districts within the states must have school board–approved bullying policies. As a classroom teacher, be sure you are aware of the specific policy in your state or district and follow it to the letter. Parents reading this book, inquire as to the specific policy that is in place for your child's district. Administrators reading this book, please take time to make all personnel aware of all components of the district policy. Note: Private schools vary on bullying policies. If you are associated with a private school, you will need to take the initiative to find out the specifics of the policy—if it exists.

After reading the previous paragraphs, you are probably recalling your own life experiences. Soon you will be naming names also. You can easily see the contrast between male and female bullies. Boys are aggressive and physically violent. They threaten to beat others up if they don't do as the bully says. Male bullies are so easily obvious to classroom teachers. We can see this behavior. Girls go for the jugular by isolating, ostracizing, and withdrawing from their victims socially. Female bullies may threaten to "not like them" or to "not play with them" or to "not be friends" as a result of their antagonism.

Some studies completed in early childhood settings are now showing that female bullies exist as early as preschool and kindergarten. Female bullies start young and perfect their craft over time. Female bullying often goes unnoticed by the classroom teacher. She or he may view the victims as a tattletales because someone *said* he or she wouldn't play with them. We're not social directors, we're teachers! In reality, we are interested in the whole child, in social as well as cognitive development. It is the teacher's job to create a learning environment beneficial to all students. Teachers need to be aware of all forms of bullying and make adjustments to stop it. As Barney Fife would say, "Nip it in the bud." The fact that 88 to 90 percent of classroom teachers are female is an advantage in thwarting female bullying. Teachers should be able to spot and nip female bullying.

HEARING—BOYS VERSUS GIRLS

Girls are born with a fantastic ability to hear. Some studies have shown that female fetuses hear better than male fetuses. If we as classroom teachers know this fact, what changes in our instructional strategies and classroom routines can we make to best assist the boys?

One obvious change would be to seat the boys near or at the front of the classroom. A soft-spoken teacher is not reaching the back of the classroom with her or his voice. Other noise factors in the classroom, such as heating and cooling appliances, also make it difficult for the students to hear the classroom teacher. Because the vast majority of teachers are female—with softer voices—boys are also at a disadvantage hearing the teacher. A simple rearrangement of classroom seating will help all students hear vital instructions and directions.

CLASSROOM MANAGEMENT—BOYS VERSUS GIRLS

Girls are quieter in class and tend toward sedentary behavior, according to Gurian and Ballew (2003). Boys, on the other hand, are louder in class and more physically active. Boys are more competitive than girls. Boys are more prone to attention-getting classroom behaviors than girls.

In preschool and kindergarten, boys make up between 80 and 90 percent of discipline problems (Gurian and Ballew, 2003). In other grades, boys cause 90 percent of the discipline problems in school. These are huge statistics! The previous section suggested moving boys to the front of the classroom so that they can hear well. The teacher could also move the boys to the front of the room in an attempt to reduce the percentage of discipline problems. Keeping these statistics in mind when setting up a classroom or learning environment will help the instructor take a proactive approach.

ACADEMICS—BOYS VERSUS GIRLS

Gurian and Ballew (2003) state what teachers have known for generations—boys do better in math and science, and girls do better in reading and language arts. They do specify the degree of advancement: "girls are approximately one and a half years ahead of boys in reading and writing competence at all school levels" (p. 24). One and a half years is considered light years at the elementary level. Think about all the "read-the-text-and-answer-the-questions-(write) assignments given in classrooms (which does not appeal to the various learning styles). Now revisit that idea remembering that the male student population is considerably behind in those skills. Perhaps this contributes to the attention-getting misbehaviors and discipline problems among frustrated male students.

Veteran educators will say that students learn by doing—these are the folks who provide kinesthetic learning opportunities for the students to achieve long-term learning, learning[2]. This 18-month gap in proficiency between male and female students can be improved with practice. Yes, practice and some super instructional strategies. One of the easiest strategies is to go over the questions *before* reading the text. This is such a simple change, but the student then has a purpose for reading the text. (This is also a great test-taking strategy to use with reading questions on standardized tests.)

Another easy strategy is to give some advance information about the text content prior to having the students read. Make every attempt to make the assignment relevant to the students. Not many 7-year-olds are thrilled about reading about pandas living in China. What if you told them that pandas are not really bears? They are part of a family very close to the raccoons. It seems that raccoons are sort of like a cousin to pandas. "How many of you have cousins? How many of you have ever seen a raccoon? How big were they? Did they have unique color markings? Well, pandas also have unique color markings. Today we will go over our questions. I especially want you to read the text to find out which is larger, the panda or the raccoon." Now these second graders are pumped and ready to read.

They have a purpose. The text is relevant to them. One final note on this scenario: You *always* tell the students what to do with their assignment after they are finished. For example, "When you are finished today please put your paper in your reading folder." As many times a day as assignments are given, students still will waste time asking or wondering what to do after they are finished.

It seems that this read-and-answer-questions-(write) scenario is prevalent in subject areas other than reading or language arts. This is often the bread-and-butter assignment given in science and social studies classes. You are reading this and disagreeing because students *should* be experiencing highly kinesthetic learning activities in these subjects. Remember that 46-35-19 (46 visual, 35 kinesthetic, 19 auditory) breakdown from Sousa (1998) in chapter 1? These are two subjects for which to bring out the manipulatives and let them learn by doing. The supplements to the textbooks in these areas are basically the fill-in-the-blank assignments to be used after reading the text. Gurian and Ballew remind us that read-and-write assignments are to the female students' advantage. The previous section reminds us that 90 percent of all discipline problems come from male students. Sousa's breakdown of learning styles also shows that the read-and-write assignments are not beneficial to all learning styles. Therefore, as the educational leader of your enriched learning environment, consider instructional strategies that lead to learning for *both* genders, for *all* students. (Administrators, please reread this paragraph. As the curriculum leader of your school site and the person who deals with many of the disruptions, this is powerful information for you.)

According to Gurian and Ballew (2003, p. 23), "at the high school level, girls receive approximately 60 percent of the A's." On the other hand, boys at the high school level receive approximately 70 percent of the D's and F's. This is classroom performance on daily assignments and exams. Again, could adjustments in classroom instruction change these statistics?

The 1.5-year gap between boys and girls widens as the students continue through school. According to the United States Department of Education, "the average eleventh-grade American boy now writes at the same level as the average eighth-grade girl" (U.S. Department of Education, 2000, p. 18). The 1.5-year gap doubles to 3 years over time. Educators, administrators, and parents can work together to shrink that gap and, hopefully, eliminate it entirely.

LEARNING PROBLEMS—BOYS VERSUS GIRLS

Sax (2005) makes the point throughout his book that many students diagnosed with attention deficit disorder and attention deficit disorder with hyperactivity are misdiagnosed. They are the victims of poor instructional decisions by the teacher. They are students of teachers who do not understand the differences between boys and girls. With proper planning and unique instructional strategies, this group of students would not display the behaviors associated with ADD and ADHD.

Statistically, 20 percent of children diagnosed with ADHD or ADD are females (Gurian and Ballew, 2003). Therefore, 80 percent of all diagnosed ADHD and ADD students are male. This is an incredible statistic for parents, teachers, and administrators. The age-old question of "Why?" instantly comes to mind. If you ask teachers or physicians, the answers will vary. No concrete answer comes to the forefront. It is still a phenomenal difference in male and female students. Parents, teachers, administrators, and physicians need to take a long, hard look at the "Why?" question and find a sound answer.

According to Gurian and Ballew (2003), "We (Americans) medicate earlier than in Europe and use 80 percent of the world's Ritalin" (p. 124). Gurian and Ballew did not use the term "Wow!" after that statement in their book. However, I will. Wow! Forget how much money insurance companies and American families are spending monthly on prescriptions for children with ADHD or ADD. Forget the profit that major pharmaceutical companies are making per year by manufacturing and distributing Ritalin and similar drugs. American children and adolescents consuming 80 percent of the world's Ritalin is staggering, astonishing, alarming, concerning, shocking, and every other "-ing" word in the thesaurus. Again, *wow!*

Two thirds, 66 percent, of all learning-disabled students are male. Two out of three children diagnosed as learning disabled are male. Again, that is an overwhelming ratio. And the reason is—not yet determined. A very good educated guess is that the 18-month delay in the area of reading and writing is connected in some way. According to Gurian and Ballew (2003), "most special education and learning disorders occur after age six, and many learning diagnoses are based on cultural expectations. Because males have a disadvantage in early reading, many in the U.S. are diagnosed with learning disorders" (p. 134).

EDUCATIONAL TREND—SINGLE-GENDER CLASSES

Over 50 years ago, the U.S. Supreme Court ruled on the *Brown v. the Board of Topeka* case. They found that separate was not equal. Briefly, the Brown family believed that their daughter, Linda, was not receiving the same education as students attending an all-Caucasian school. Thurgood Marshall, prior to becoming a Supreme Court justice, argued on behalf of the Brown family.

This monumental educational case about segregation was followed in 1972 by Title IX. Basically, Title IX prohibits sex-based discrimination in schools. Brown stated that we cannot discriminate by race or segregate by race. Title IX states that we cannot discriminate by sex. How, then, can we have single-gender classes?

New legislation passed in 2001 legalized single-sex education in American public schools. This legislation was written by Senator Kay Hutchinson and Senator Hillary Clinton. The Senate unanimously approved this proposal. This means that educators have flexibility to provide more options. Physical education and sex education classes could be single-sex classes before this legislation. Now educators can choose other offerings for students. Because this is a new educational trend, parents and students will also have the choice of participating in these classes.

This chapter has been enlightening and insightful. Many long-time educators and administrators have suspected some of these findings. The facts and figures may confirm their anticipations. If you are a homeschool parent, perhaps you are educating your children in a single-sex environment already. If you are a community volunteer, this information will be helpful to you when you prepare and plan the learning opportunities for children. Many situations, such as scouting or various religious instructions, already have same-sex learning environments. Many, however, do not. Hopefully you will be best prepared to educate the children in your charge.

- Summary for administrators: Make the bullying policy available to all personnel. Continue to update faculty with professional development speakers and conferences to help them stay current on trends and signs of bullying. Encourage your personnel to nip bullying in the bud.

  Take a look at the statistics for males and females in the special services programs at your school site. Are they as disproportionate as the national statistics? Discuss possible reasons with the special services teachers at your site.

  I hope you shared a "wow" moment with someone when reading the information on ADD/ADHD. What is the percentile of students at your school taking medication for ADHD or ADD? Do you keep those statistics each year? You might compare them with statistics from other school sites within your district or region. What can be done as a school-wide effort to reduce the numbers of students on medication? As the curricular leader of your school site, would your faculty benefit from professional development of current, cutting-edge educational strategies to use with students? Is there a possibility that some students would not need medication if lessons were designed to utilize all three learning styles?

- Summary for teachers: The differences for males and females in this chapter are staggering. Your special services teachers will be a good resource to you when you attempt to determine if students have potential learning disabilities.

  Be aware of bullying tendencies. Abide by the district or site policy. You might want to include an antibullying rule along with your classroom rules. Work to educate parents and provide a copy of the bullying policy to every household.

What changes can you make to provide your students with lessons that appeal to the three learning styles? Would this have an impact on potential ADD/ADHD students?

- Summary for religious and community volunteers: I hope this chapter has been enlightening to you. Please continue to stay current with your readings about genders. A good resource for you would be your area public school. The teachers and administrators should be able to answer your questions.

    You may already be working with children in a same-sex environment. Be aware of the characteristics of males and females presented in this chapter.

- Summary for homeschool parents: You may also be teaching in a same-sex environment. Hopefully, you do not have any problem with bullying.

    The information about ADD/ADHD is staggering. Make every attempt to select lessons that appeal to all three learning styles. Throughout the book, creative and innovative curricular suggestions are made that will work with your child.

REFERENCES

Gurian, M., & Ballew, A. (2003). *The boys and girls learn differently action guide for teachers*. San Francisco, CA: Jossey-Bass.

Sax, L. (2005). *Why gender matters: What parents and teachers need to know about the emerging science of sex differences*. New York: Doubleday.

Sousa, D. (1998). *How the brain learns: More new insights for educators*. A presentation on August 18, 1998, Port Washington, WI.

U.S. Department of Education. (2000). *Educational equity for girls and women*. Washington, DC: U.S. Government Printing Office.

II

HOW CAN WE
IMPROVE LEARNING?

4

INCREASE OXYGEN

Learning is a treasure that will follow its owner everywhere.

—Chinese proverb

Education is not the filling of a pail, but the lighting of a fire.

—W. B. Yeats

Every book or article you read on brain research will discuss the simple changes that can be made to the very simplest human necessities. These changes can dramatically affect the student's academic performance, overall health and well-being, and behavior at school.

The educator reading this chapter will see ways in which oxygen can be incorporated into the daily classroom environment. You can regulate this at school. The aspects of sleeping and eating are choices that are made by the student and parents at home. The administrator will see the importance of oxygen in the workplace and the learning environment. These suggestions can be incorporated into professional development for the entire faculty and staff. The parent and community volunteer will understand and be able to make necessary changes in the study location or meeting place for optimum learning for children. The teacher education candidate will be sensitive to the value of oxygen when making observations in school and also during clinical practice or student teaching.

The values of proper nutrition and sleep are also vital to the student. Although this area is not regulated by the school, their importance is also paramount to the student's academic well-being and health. The school, and more specifically the classroom teacher, can educate families and students about their importance and value.

Oxygen is vital to the human body. The brain uses one fifth of the total oxygen supply used by the body. The most obvious suggestion to individuals working with children is to open the windows prior to the school day to allow fresh air to fill the classroom. As a former classroom teacher, I understand that the windows do not stay open, not all the windows have screens, some are painted shut, and so on. During the colder months of the year, it is not cost-effective to allow cold air to fill the classroom. Many new schools are being designed with windows that do not open. This is the case in many office buildings, hospitals, universities today.

If for some reason the obvious opening of windows is not possible or practical, we need a Plan B. If we cannot bring fresh air into the classroom through the windows, perhaps we can create some fresh air through the use of live plants. When I was a classroom teacher, I had several plants around my classroom. I often knocked the dust from the plastic leaves. They looked great and never needed water. Artificial plants are not the solution—you need *live* plants in your classroom or learning environment. According to Jensen (1995), "The best plants for optimal pollutant reduction, oxygen and enhancing indoor learning environments are: ficus benjamina, philodendrons, dracaena deremensis, peace lilies, bamboo palms, yellow chrysanthemums, and gerbera daisies" (p. 314). Other studies have recommended chrysanthemums of any color. Let's translate Jensen's botanical terms into laymen's terms. The best plants to produce oxygen in your classroom/meeting room are ficus, philodendrons, dracaenas, peace lilies, small palms, mums, and gerbera daisies (colored daisies).

The inquisitive reader will be asking, "How many plants do I need for my classroom?" According to Jensen (1995), "A single plant can often affect 100 square feet of space" (p. 314). Refreshing your mathematical skills, you multiply the length of your classroom by the width of your classroom to find the square footage. Depending on the size of your room, you may need more than one plant for your room. You may choose to use a variety of the plants recommended above.

I also recommend that you contact your local greenhouse or nursery for their suggestions for plants in your area that are high oxygen producers. Depending on the region of the country in which you live, you may have some regional plants that will easily adapt to your room. I strongly suggest that you specify that you want plants that are nonpoisonous to humans yet provide optimal oxygen for your room. An administrator reading this book could make the call and create a table or chart for distribution to the entire faculty. That would save time for individual teachers—valuable time that can be spent on other classroom necessities.

Many of you reading this book may think it is humorous that I would suggest that we need nonpoisonous plants in schools and meeting rooms. No child is going to be eating a ficus or philodendron salad! Never underestimate the inquisitive nature of students. Make every effort to prepare a safe learning environment for all students. You are the adult in charge. Student safety is paramount.

If you have a ceiling fan in your room, this is a great way to distribute the oxygen generated by the plants you choose for your room. If you have a central heating and cooling unit in your room, consider setting it on the fan setting for 5 to 10 minutes and let it circulate the oxygenated air. A final suggestion is to remember to close your classroom door during recess times, lunch time, and after school. You will be able to keep that wonderfully oxygenated air *in* the room, rather than allowing it to flow into the hallway.

- Summary for administrators: Work with your faculty and staff to bring in oxygenating plants to the school site. Do you have one in your office? Set the standard for others to follow. You are the curricular and educational leader of your school site. What changes can be made in the school office area to help your administrative assistants have oxygenated air?
- Summary for teachers: Consider ways in which you can bring oxygen into the enriched learning environment you have worked

so hard to create for your students. Use nonpoisonous high-oxy-genating plants in the classrooms to provide a wonderful learn-ing environment for the students. Work with the janitorial staff to keep the door of your classroom closed when they are clean-ing after school. Leave directions in your substitute folder to keep the door closed when the children are at recess or lunch. Make every effort to bring in the oxygen and keep it in your classroom.

- Summary for community and religious volunteers: Be sure you have enough lighting and moderate 24/7 temperatures before selecting your nonpoisonous plants for your meeting room. Post a note on the door to keep the door shut.
- Summary for homeschool parents: Place nonpoisonous high-oxygenating plants in your child's room so he or she will re-ceive the benefits 24/7. Also consider placing these plants throughout your home as well.

REFERENCE

Jensen, E. (1995). *The learning brain.* San Diego, CA: Turning Point Pub-lishing.

5

INCREASE
WATER INTAKE

The mediocre teacher tells. The good teacher explains. The superior teacher demonstrates. The great teacher inspires.

—William Arthur Ward

The brain weighs approximately 3 pounds. Its primary composition is water. The brain needs water to successfully complete all its functions on a daily basis. As humans, we prefer many beverages rather than water. Remember, our brain is composed primarily of water—not sugary manufactured drinks; therefore, it needs water rather than those manufactured drinks.

Individuals who are lethargic, sluggish, bored, droopy, or listless may, in fact, be dehydrated. In many cases, elementary students who complain of headaches are dehydrated rather than ill. Some researchers believe that the average learner is dehydrated.

Aside from lethargy, sluggishness, and boredom, dehydration can cause stress. As the percentage of water in the blood decreases, the salt level increases. Increased salt levels can cause the feelings of tenseness and stress. Stress researchers found that within 5 minutes of drinking water, there is a marked decline in the hormones that elevate stress (Jensen, 1998).

As a classroom teacher, parent, or volunteer working with children, please provide ways in which children can drink water frequently throughout the day. The body requires water throughout the day to boost attention and reduce stress symptoms. Quantities differ depending on the size of the child, as well as the weather conditions.

If you are the only classroom teacher at your school site that encourages the use of water throughout the day, discuss this with your principal and seek administrative approval. Send home a letter to the parents notifying them of your policy. Consider possible rules for bringing water to school.

An obvious rule would be allowing only plastic bottles, rather than allowing the children to transport glass containers to school. Student safety is paramount. You may wish to allow only clear containers for bringing water to class. You may also wish to ask the students to be on the honor system. Because there are so many beverages available that are clear, by asking the students to be honorable you have created a safety net by trusting the students to bring only water in the containers. Notify the parents of your honor system so they are aware in writing that only water is permitted on a daily basis in your classroom.

Another matter is having the child's name on the bottle. This will prevent children from sharing bottles and, therefore, sharing germs. Please notify the parents in writing that they need to be sure the student's name is on the bottle prior to sending it to school. This will prevent problems at the beginning of the day when the classroom teacher has a zillion items on the To Do list and he or she has to stop and add one more item to the list.

Other potential problems are students sharing their bottles with others. Although we encourage sharing at school, this is not a situation in which sharing is required. Explain to the students why they should not share their water. You might also explain to them that they need to change the bottles often for sanitation purposes. Think through all possible problems before you write down your policy, notify the administration, and notify the parents.

John Dewey wrote and spoke about "teachable moments." Use the benefits of drinking water as a lesson or unit for your students. Turn this practice into a teachable moment.

Practice what you preach. Leave the coffee, tea, and soft drinks at home. If you are encouraging your students to drink water, they need to see you "getting with the program." Be a living and breathing role model.

- Summary for administrators: Encourage your entire faculty to start a schoolwide focus on students and staff hydrating throughout the day. Remember that dehydration is more frequent during cold weather when individuals are subjected to forced-air heating systems. If you live in an area that is very dry, consider purchasing humidifiers for the classrooms as part of the school budget.
- Summary for teachers: Work with your parents to have them send water each day for the students. Consider asking the district or parent organization to purchase humidifiers for your classroom to use during cold weather. Set an example for your students and other faculty by bringing water each day.
- Summary for religious and community volunteers: Rather than soda pop or sugary juice drinks, consider offering water to the students during each meeting/session.
- Summary for homeschool parents: Encourage your child to drink water throughout the day.

REFERENCE

Jensen, E. (1998). *Teaching with the brain in mind.* Alexandria, VA: Association for Supervision & Curriculum Development.

6

IMPROVE NUTRITION

One mark of a great educator is the ability to lead students out to new places where even the educator has never been.

—Thomas Groome

The best teachers teach from the heart, not from the book.

—Author unknown

Educators have known for years that proper nutrition promotes a healthy student. Proper nutrition begins with the first meal of the day—breakfast. Teachers, administrators, parents, and also students who miss breakfast have started the day off on the wrong foot. The old term *short on groceries* can be used to describe an individual who arrives at school without breakfast.

"Students who eat a nutritious breakfast make fewer errors throughout the morning than those who skip breakfast" (Given, 1998, p. 70). The "errors" discussed by Given can be academic errors as well as behavioral errors. Educators hope to alleviate both types of errors in the classroom; therefore, teachers and administrators should work with parents to encourage children to eat breakfast before coming to school.

Along with encouraging your students to bring water to school each day, consider encouraging your students to bring a healthy snack to school for midmorning or midafternoon. According to Given, "Although the availability of appropriate foods could have a positive impact on student learning and behavior, schools rarely provide snacks or encourage parents to do so. Without question, many students could profit from having access to healthful snacks throughout the school day, or at least at midmorning" (Given, 1998, pp. 70–71). According to Jensen (1995), "Too much time in between eating can cause loss of concentration and decreased alertness" (p. 158). We can translate Jensen's statement to mean that snacking will improve concentration and alertness in the classroom. Jensen (1995) continues these thoughts. "Adolescents were given a choice of either snacking and nibbling during a test or not eating at all. Those who were permitted to eat the snacks (popcorn or raw vegetables) achieve 'significantly higher' scores than the group who was not allowed to nibble" (p. 158). Erlauer also supports the use of snacks for better school achievement.

> While a bias may be to treasure the big, established dinnertime for the value of conversation between family members, several small, healthy snacks during the day are good for the body and the brain. Allowing students a quick healthy snack midmorning and even again midafternoon can give them a bit more energy to pay attention to lessons. (Erlauer, 2003, p. 41)

Educators, administrators, and parents want students who are concentrating and alert in our classrooms. This is a great win-win situation for everyone.

Many schools offer a breakfast or lunch program that the student can utilize. As a classroom teacher, consider working with your school food service director about the possibility of offering an inexpensive midmorning or midafternoon snack for your students. If the school offers this option, the student can purchase the snack and the school will keep track of all the paperwork. The food service department will take care of refrigerating the snack, if necessary. You will know that the snack has been prepared in a hygienic working environment under the proper public health standards. A possible Plan B would be to purchase milk from the cafeteria in substitution for a snack. This would be cost-effective for all students. The school would keep track of the money and also the milk inventory and storage.

Another option is to work with the parents about sending a snack with the student. The parent will be aware of any food allergies or any dietary problems, which is a major concern of teachers. Again, student safety is paramount. Rather than ask the teacher to keep tabs on every child and every allergy, the parents would be responsible.

Keep in mind that a snack is good for the student. Keep in mind also that the teacher is pulled as thin as phyllo dough each day. No extra duties need to be piled onto the classroom teacher. By asking the food service department to provide the snack or by working with the parents, the burden of responsibility is off the shoulders of the classroom teacher.

Just as proper planning is needed when you encourage students to bring water to class, advanced planning is required before snacking becomes a reality in the classroom. "When" and "where" are good issues to examine. If you have a diabetic student in your class, consider having your snack time the same time that student will be eating his or her snack. Also consider your daily schedule before setting the time. The students may be so busy during the morning that the most practical time of day is the afternoon. Another support of the afternoon snack is that so many students have another agenda after school in the form of either a practice, a club meeting, or going on to a day care facility. They may not be eating supper or dinner till after 7:00 P.M. The afternoon snack would be beneficial to students in that category. Examine all the possibilities before making a final decision.

The big question of "where" needs to be examined with the lowest level of stress in the classroom taken into consideration. I once taught in a school that did not have a cafeteria. The students ate lunch at their desks in the classroom. They were responsible for using a sponge to clean off the desks before and after lunch. My room also smelled like the lunch entrée for the remainder of the day if I didn't open the classroom windows. Many schools still lack a cafeteria and must optimize existing space.

Classroom teachers do not need to add the role of janitor to their repertoire. Design your snack so that a classroom helper passes out napkins or paper towels. Assign students to pass the trash after snack time. Be prepared in advance if the desks need to be cleaned before and after snacks. Also consider a philosophy that no food touches the desk. The container will obviously touch, but not the contents. With this philosophy in mind, parents will be mindful when selecting the snack for school.

If the school food service department is responsible for snacks, the students may eat their snack in a location other than the classroom. They will have cafeteria guidelines to follow.

We have examined the when and where questions. What are good nutrition choices for students to have as a snack at school? There are many days when I can give a great debate to support a can of pop and a candy bar that I really want to eat. Pop and candy are not the best food choices for students—or teachers—no matter how much we want to eat them. According to Given, some suggestions might include "bagels, graham crackers, popcorn, bread sticks, granola bars, vanilla wafers, melba toast, raw vegetables, or other carbohydrates" (1998, p. 71). Other possible snacks might include crackers and peanut butter, beef jerky, or trail mix. Keep in mind the philosophy that no food touches the desk; the above-mentioned snacks can be eaten from a bag, paper plate, paper towel, or coffee filter. Coffee filters are extremely inexpensive and cost-effective. Other food choices such as canned fruits (peaches, pears, oranges) can be eaten from the can, but the parent is responsible for sending a spoon or fork for their child.

When considering which snacks are appropriate for school, student safety is paramount. Because the teacher does not have access to a refrigerator to store snacks such as yogurt, parents need to share your concern regarding food spoilage and possible food poisoning. Certain vegetables such as carrots, celery, and zucchini are great snacks, but their quality diminishes when left at room temperature for several hours. Eating a limp, room-temperature carrot stick is not very appetizing or exciting.

Just as the students are on the honor system when bringing water to school, the teacher could use the honor system when including snacks during the day. Leftover snacks will promote infestations of insects and mice at school. Leftovers need to be tossed or returned home rather than stuffed inside desks or lockers. Students need and deserve a clean working space and a clean classroom. Students need to practice hygiene.

Just as sharing water is not allowed, students need to eat only what they have brought. Educators are always encouraging students to share in various social situations. Drinking water and eating food are not in this league—no sharing in this area!

Just as the teacher designs guidelines prior to bringing water to school, guidelines for food need to be well considered. Involve your administrator in the planning phase so that you have his or her support. After the parameters have been calculated, notify your parents in writing. Use this as a John Dewey "teachable moment" to educate your students about the benefits of proper nutrition. Another topic for a teachable moment is to sanitize hands before snacking. Children are encouraged to wash their hands before eating lunch. It would be difficult to stop instruction for a hand-washing break before snacks. Is there an alternative? This could be achieved by asking the children to have sanitizing wipes or gel in their school box to use before snacking. With so many germs around us in an enriched learning environment each day, taking time to sanitize hands will help to stop the spread of germs.

Be a role model and bring nutritious snacks to class each day. You will see the benefits for yourself as well as for your students. According to Jensen (1997), "The brain runs best on a more consistent 'nibbling diet'" (p. 59). Medically, "nibblers maintained a better insulin level, had lower cortical levels and better glucose tolerance. These indicators can lead to better cognitive functioning, fewer discipline problems and an enhanced sense of well-being" (Jensen, 1995, p. 158). These are all valid reasons to share with parents and the administration when explaining your rationale for encouraging students to snack during the school day.

- Summary for administrators: Encourage your entire faculty to start a schoolwide focus on students and staff nibbling or snacking. Set the school example by bringing nutritious snacks for yourself.

Work with the food service program at your school site about the possibility of an extra milk or a snack each day for children. Could children who receive free or reduced lunches also receive free or reduced milk or snacks? Search out the possibilities. Children will benefit from your efforts.

Work with the janitorial staff and faculty about an efficient cleanup routine. Help to establish a policy to be shared with parents and students. Leftovers can bring unwanted guests into your school.

- Summary for teachers: Work with your parents to provide a snack each day for the students. Select the time of day that is best for your students. Keep in mind the after-school schedules of your students as well as the lunch schedule.
- Summary for religious and community volunteers: Rather than cookies or sugary snacks, consider offering one of the food suggestions from this chapter for the students during each meeting or session.
- Summary for homeschool parents: You are aware of any food allergies your child might have. Set a time for a midmorning and midafternoon snack for your child. Use the suggestions from this chapter for ideas for snacks.

REFERENCES

Erlauer, L. (2003). *The brain-compatible classroom: Using what we know about learning to improve teaching.* Alexandria, VA: Association for Supervision and Curriculum Development.

Given, B. (1998). Food for thought. *Educational Leadership, 56*(3), 68–71.

Jensen, E. (1995). *The learning brain.* San Diego, CA: Turning Point Publishing.

Jensen, E. (1997). *Brain compatible strategies.* San Diego, CA: Turning Point Publishing.

7

INCREASE EXERCISE
AND MOVEMENT

Teachers who inspire realize there will always be rocks in the road ahead of us. They will be stumbling blocks or stepping stones; it all depends on how we use them.

—Author unknown

Today's children have become a sedentary generation. Society's children are watching television and playing video games rather than running and playing outside after school. We have a "screen generation" watching entertainment on screens ranging from the size of a watch face to that of a big-screen television. Computer screens have also entered the life of children—both at home and at school. Students don't move while watching entertainment, playing games, or sitting in front of a computer screen—they sit still.

This stagnation in lifestyle has led to serious health problems, and at the top of the list is childhood obesity, which is reaching epidemic levels.

In a classroom of 20 American school children, four are now overweight or obese—twice the number 25 years ago. Seven of the children in that classroom will be obese as adults, and some may suffer heart attacks as early as age 30. If we continue to follow the current food and fitness trends, in 15 years 75 percent of Americans will be overweight. ("Where Can Your Kids Stay Fit and Healthy?" 2005)

Parents play a big role in promoting a healthy and active lifestyle as well as providing a healthy diet for children. Schools also play a role. Many elementary schools are promoting student physical activity by providing physical education classes. A 2005 study ranked the states. The top 10 are (1) Connecticut, (2) New York, (3) Vermont, (4) Massachusetts, (5) Missouri, (6) Maine, (7) West Virginia, (8) Wisconsin, (9) Arkansas, and (10) Illinois.

The lowest scoring states all have common factors: No mandatory PE classes, no nutrition classes, little sports, and lots of junk food ("Where Can Your Kids," 2005). The 10 lowest scoring states on the study were (41) Iowa, (42) Wyoming, (43) Idaho, (44) Alabama, (45) South Dakota, (46) Kansas, (47) Mississippi, (48) Nevada, and (49) Nebraska. The 50th-ranking was Alaska. According to the study, "the state (Alaska) only requires physical education for high-school students. As for elementary schools, even when it's offered, about 85 percent of classes are taught by regular teachers instead of specialists. Alaska also has poor safety ratings on its playgrounds." (Cicero, 2005).

The physical benefits of exercise to the body are well known. Exercise also benefits the brain. Neuroscientists have discovered that the brain's cerebellum, involved in most learning, operates at high capacity during times of movement, according to Erlauer (2003). One Canadian study found that of 500 students, those who spend 1 extra hour per day in a physical education class scored higher on examinations than did those who did not have increased movement. The results also showed that with participation in frequent aerobic exercise, the students increased their reaction time, creativity, and short-term memory, according to Sylwester (1995).

As a classroom teacher, I often took my class out for a "fresh air break." We would leave our classroom, leave the building, and walk around the building, then return to the rest of our day's agenda. I could see the students slipping away. I could see that they were lethargic and listless. (I was beginning to sound like the teacher in the Charlie Brown cartoons!) Instead of giving a 5-minute nap time, I got them up, got fresh air in their lungs, and got them moving.

Classroom teachers, please consider the weather when rounding up your students for an "oxygen regenerator" such as this. Icy sidewalks, lightning, and other weather-related problems will prompt educators to postpone this idea for another day with better weather conditions.

Another tactic I frequently used was a stretch time. We would have stretches while sitting at our desks. We stretched everything that had been overused due to writing and prolonged sitting. We stretched our hands and fingers, our ankles and toes, our knees, and our jaws and necks. We even did an eyebrow stretch in which the students had to listen and distinguish between their left and right eyebrow or at least try to do so. Finally, we would stand up for body stretches. After sitting at a desk for a long period of time, everyone— no matter the age—can benefit from standing and stretching. According to Erlauer (2003),

> Just standing up can increase the blood flow in the human body, bringing more oxygen to the brain. The increased oxygen gives the brain more energy and reduces stress, and it promotes the production of hormones that enhance the growth and strengthen the connections between the brain cells. (pp. 45–46)

Erlauer (2003) discusses a teacher who used small beanbags at each student's desk. The students tossed the beanbags from one hand to another as they counted in math. This idea can be used in spelling by asking the students to transfer the beanbag from hand to hand as they spell the letters of the words aloud. It would be great for saying various math "fact families" aloud. Language arts students can toss the beanbags from hand to hand while conjugating verbs. Social studies students can toss the beanbags when reciting the states and capitals or countries of a continent and their capitals or reciting the presidents of the United States in order—George Washington, John Adams, Thomas Jefferson, and so on. The same tactic could be used with the days of the week, months of the year, and other concepts. It could also be used with the same concepts learned in a foreign language. The use of small beanbags has potential in all curriculum areas. They are also very inexpensive to make. The teacher could sew the beanbags from fabric and fill them with rice or beans. A second easy way to make beanbags is to put beans or rice inside a small resealable plastic bag. The latter is very time-efficient. Consider putting the small resealable bag inside another resealable bag for extra reinforcement—double-bag them to avoid one bag bursting. I have used the resealable bags as beanbags to toss on a large United States map. The students were asked to tell the name of the state or the capital of that state on which the beanbag was located. Although this was a verbal activity, it could have been a paper-and-pencil activity as well.

Movement involves stretching, exercising, and relocating. Consider having the first part of the lesson in one location and moving the class to another location for the remainder of the lesson. This change in location, or relocation, involves a small transition that allows students to stand, stretch, and move. According to Erlauer (2003), "Movement in terms of changing locations can also cause a marked improvement in memory" (p. 46). Erlauer also states that students' memories can be improved when they move to a different location to learn something new.

All educators, parents, and administrators want an improvement in students' memories. Consider the layout of your classroom or work area. How can you add a movement transition in that area? Also consider areas other than inside the classroom. Set up your classroom with centers, areas for group work, and entire-group work. A great idea is to use carpet samples for each child to sit on if you don't have space for a carpet or rug. These can be obtained from numerous carpet and tile retail stores that are willing to donate outdated samples. The advantages of carpet samples include easy storage and no cost to the school; they can be rearranged each time you use them, and when they are damaged or worn they can be tossed in the trash. You can give a prompt during a future lesson by telling the students, "Remember when we sat on the rug and I told you about the Boston Tea Party?" That verbal cue will prompt the students to mentally return to the story that was told in that location.

Parents and homeschool parents can take the students outside for a lesson or study time. My mother often had my son bounce a basketball to practice his spelling words. He would make one bounce per letter. This could also be done with a volleyball, a tennis ball, a golf ball, a basketball, or a soccer ball. Students can also combine location with movement while reciting definitions, listing continents, states, capitals, or presidents in order, or saying math facts aloud— 6 (bounce) times 4 (bounce) equals 24 (bounce). The ball can also be bounced between two people. Another suggestion is to use a jump rope rather than a ball. Consider a Chinese jump rope rather than the traditional style. It can be used inside as well as outside. It also requires a small amount of space.

- Summary for administrators: Encourage your teachers to implement forward-thinking, ahead-of-the-times ways to get and keep students moving. Read the study cited on the Internet. What improvements can you make at your school site to promote physical activity for every child every day?

  Is your school site in one of the top 10 states? Are you perhaps in one of the bottom 10 states? What improvements can you make to help the students improve mobility and movement throughout the day?
- Summary for teachers: Take your students on a fresh air break. Allow stretch time several times each day—even if it's just the eyebrows. Get them to stand up for a while throughout the day. Bring in bean bags, a stress ball, things to keep them stationary but busy. Small changes in your daily routine will help increase their attention and improve learning.
- Summary for community and religious volunteers: Because you have a limited time to work with the students, allow them some movement time before you settle down for your lessons. Consider their day prior to being with you. They may have been seated at a desk in school the entire day. A few minutes of physical movement will pay off greatly.
- Summary for homeschool parents: Utilize the suggestions from this chapter with your child during instruction/work time.

REFERENCES

Cicero, K. (2005, April). The 10 best and worst states for fit kids. Retrieved June 7, 2006, from www.child.com/kids/health_nutrition/fittest_states.jsp.

Erlauer, L. (2003). *The brain-compatible classroom: Using what we know about learning to improve teaching.* Alexandria, VA: Association for Supervision and Curriculum Development.

Sylwester, R. (1995). *A celebration of neurons: An educator's guide to the human brain.* Alexandria, VA: Association for Supervision and Curriculum Development.

Where can your kids stay fit and healthy? (2005). Retrieved April 10, 2006, from www.msnbc.msn.com/id/7137441/.

8

USE COLOR

There is no more noble profession than teaching. A great teacher is a great artist, but his medium is not canvas, but the human soul.

—Author unknown

Every child is an artist. The problem is how to remain an artist once he grows up.

—Pablo Ruiz y Picasso

How important are the visual arts in our society? I feel strongly that the visual arts are of vast and incalculable importance. Of course I could be prejudiced. I am a visual art.

—Kermit the Frog

If apple is the language of the future, then art must be the core.

—Elliot W. Eisner

Perhaps you turned to this chapter just to see if there was a typing error in the title. No, the title is correct. Using color in your daily classroom instruction *can* improve student learning. Color can boost memory retention by up to 20 percent. Some studies have also suggested that students learn the material faster when color is incorporated into the lessons. If it means they learn it faster and retain it longer, color is an important asset to the enriched learning environment. Suggestions are made in this chapter to easily incorporate colors into the learning process to promote long-term learning, learning[2].

Color can help to provide an enriched learning environment. The use of colors with various textures and patterns can spruce up your learning area. Color can be used in the bulletin boards, curtains, and various areas around the classroom.

Color can also be used during your daily routine. Organize your day's agenda by writing the morning's assignments and notes in the same color. Change color for the afternoon's information. The students will easily be able to distinguish this information. You can use colored chalk if you have a chalkboard. If you have access to a whiteboard, use erasable markers and enjoy all your color choices. I do this with adult learners every day! One great whiteboard substitute is to use a piece of "shower surround" placed on the chalkboard tray in your classroom. This is affordable and still allows the teacher to utilize the benefits of a whiteboard. The portability and easy storage are also pluses.

Always avoid using green and red in the same area. Students who are colorblind will have difficulty distinguishing these colors. Worldwide, 16 percent of males are colorblind. The racial breakdown is 8 percent Caucasian, 5 percent Asiatic, and 3 percent other. According to Swift (1997), females are also colorblind. Globally, 0.5 percent of the females from each of the Caucasian, Asiatic, and other groups are colorblind.

Teachers can also use color on overhead transparencies by using colored markers. If your transparencies are printed in black, you can still break out the markers to enhance learning. You can also create transparencies by using colored clear plastic theme or report covers. These are the ones that have the plastic spine to fit on the folded area. They can be cut with an Ellison machine or with scissors into any shape. I used them often to show fractions in math.

Elementary students can incorporate color into daily assignments. Most elementary students must write spelling words on Monday when the new words are introduced. (I hope teachers will consider introducing the new words in the middle of the week. Students will then have the weekend—some extra days—to study and really learn the words well.) Students can practice "rainbow spelling" in which they write each word using a different color. They can use colored pencils, crayons, or markers for this assignment. A spin-off of rainbow spelling is for the student to use a different color for each letter. Rather than writing the words a specific number of times, they write it only once using colors. This activity appeals to the visual and kinesthetic learners. Saying the letters as the student spells the word appeals to the auditory learner. The common practice of writing spelling words is enhanced by the use of color.

Consider having the students fill in the blanks with color. They could even circle the multiple-choice answers using a colored pencil or marker. The rainbow spelling activity could be transferred to other subjects as well. Consider using colors to write math facts. I used to teach multiplication and division by "fact families." Rather than isolate these facts, I taught them as a group—teaching multiplication and division at the same time. Three numbers were the "family." For example, 2 and 3 and 6 could be used in two multiplication and two division math sentences:

$$2 \times 3 = 6$$
$$3 \times 2 = 6$$
$$6 / 2 = 3$$
$$6 / 3 = 6$$

You could designate each number to receive a specific color. The students can see the relationships easier. Another use of color in math would be when you teach place value. Each place—the 1s, 10s, 100s, and so on—would have a different color. Using color to show place value is great when teaching decimals. Designate which color will be used for 10ths, 100ths, 1,000ths. This is especially helpful with column addition and long division. (Ask the students to turn their papers sideways for place value and column addition problems. My fifth graders loved it during long division problems. The lines are very helpful to the students.)

One of my favorite color projects involves using cake icing. In art methods class we would use three colors of icing—the primary colors—to create the secondary colors. Our "canvas" was a graham cracker or vanilla wafers. If using vanilla wafers, you can place six of them in a circle and ice the tops. The students can arrange them in order of the color wheel—three primary colors and three secondary colors. We created colorful "masterpieces" of various textures on the graham crackers. Then the adult learners ate them. Even adult learners benefit from using color and teaching lessons that appeal to the learning styles.

Cake icing can also be used as the basis for other projects. In social studies class I would give my students a cookie in the shape of Oklahoma (because that is our home state). We would ice the cookie with the cake icing. We would then add details on our "map" to show target areas within the state using various small candies and pull-apart licorice. The pull-apart licorice became the highway system or the river system. The various candies became cities, state parks, museums, and wonderful places for people to visit. After the students were finished, we then created map keys or legends of their personal maps. We also completed this project using cookies in the shape of the continental United States. Cake icing can be the backdrop for a variety of colorful class activities for your students. How can you incorporate it for math, science, language arts, and other curricular areas?

- Summary for administrators: Provide colored chalk or colored markers for your teachers as part of the office supplies. Work with the teachers to find funds for portable whiteboards if you have chalkboards installed. Provide professional development opportunities for your faculty explaining various instructional strategies that incorporate the use of color.
- Summary for teachers: Design your daily agenda using a color for the morning work and a different color for the afternoon work. Use color throughout your day in your instructional strategies.
- Summary for community and religious volunteers: Your time frame with the students is limited. Have your supplies ready to go before the students arrive.

- Summary for homeschool parents: Encourage your children to use the rainbow spelling idea as well as others that incorporate color. Get out the cake icing and food coloring and have fun!

REFERENCE

Swift, G. (1997). *Colors for the colorblind.* Retrieved April 2, 2006, from http://web.ask.com/fr?u=http%3A%2F%2Fwww.designmatrix.com%2Fp l%2Fcyberpl%2Fcftcb.html&s=a&bu=http%3A%2F%2Fweb.ask.com%2 Fweb%3Fq%3DWhat%2BPercentage%2Bof%2BPeople%2BAre%2BColor %2BBlind%26o%3D0%26page%3D1&q=What+Percentage+of+People +Are+Color+Blind&o=0&qt=0&ma=...of%20colorblind%20(color-deficient%20or%20dyschromatopic)%20people%20will%20exclude%20a %20significant%20percentage%20...%20blind%2C%20most%20peo-ple%20who%20have%20deficient%20color...&mt=Colors%20for%20the %20Colorblind&mb=7dc82236923dd28b9f621b16bc1f2ab9.

9

USE MUSIC

Teach your students to use what talents they have; the woods would be silent if no bird sang except those that sing best.

—Author unknown

Mozart has the classic purity of light and the blue ocean; Beethoven the romantic grandeur which belongs to the storms of air and sea, and while the soul of Mozart seems to dwell on the ethereal peaks of Olympus, that of Beethoven climbs shuddering the storm-beaten sides of a Sinai. Blessed be they both! Each represents a moment of the ideal life, each does us good. Our love is due to both.

—Henri Frederic Amiel

Music washes away from the soul the dust of everyday life.

—Red Auerbach

Music is a higher revelation than all wisdom and philosophy. Music is the electrical soil in which the spirit lives, thinks and invents.

—Ludwig van Beethoven

Musical intelligence is one of the eight intelligences identified by Howard Gardner. Music is not just tones—it's patterns, rhythms, volume variations, and tempos. Music is everything from Bach to Bob Wills, from Mozart to Bill Monroe. Music is part of our everyday lives. We hear music piped into our phones when we are placed on hold. Perhaps you have been a patient sitting in the dentist's chair wearing headphones listening to your choice of music. iPods allow us to tailor our music intake to our particular preference. The youngest toddlers create music by creating rhythms from various household objects. Most likely the cave men and women used the objects they had on hand to create music. Humans have been following that trend since ancient times.

The benefits of music are bountiful. "A significant positive correlation has been shown between music study and increased math, science, reading, history and SAT scores. Music listening has been shown to increase spatial-temporal reasoning, the kind of reasoning used in higher levels of math and science" (Burgess, 2000). According to information in chapter 3, music would appeal to both the male and female students. We have a heterogeneous group of students gathering in our classrooms each day, many of whom have dyslexia, listening and learning disorders, and varying degrees of attention deficit disorders, as well as many other conditions. Design innovative uses of music in your classroom or learning environment to promote learning for all students.

Which type of music is best for the learning environment and the learner? Although Bob Wills, Bill Monroe, and the Beach Boys may be at the top of our lists, according to the experts these artists are not at the top of the list for the enriched learning environment. Music from the Classical period (1750–1835) and the Romantic period (1820–1900) is better for introducing new information. Many experts recommend the works of Beethoven, Haydn, Mozart, and Handel for the learning environment.

The effect of music on young children has been studied for several years. The Mozart Effect is a term first used by Alfred A. Tomatis, who examined the effects of Mozart's works on young children. Parents and caregivers of young children soon began to expose the children to the works of Mozart, as well as other classics. I was so impressed with this fact that we started my granddaughter on a "music immersion" program when she was 3 weeks old. Every time Hailey took a nap or went to sleep for the evening, her parents played classical music in her room. The music consisted of works from Mozart, Chopin, Bach, Handel, Haydn, Vivaldi, Puccini, and Beethoven, among others. Will Hailey become a musical or mathematics whiz? Time will tell.

The idea for the Mozart Effect originated in 1993 at the University of California, Irvine. A study showed that after exposing college students to 10 minutes of music by Mozart, the students were able to increase their scores on an intelligence test. Based on this study, I play works from Mozart prior to administering tests with my adult learners. We keep the testing environment silent during the tests.

Before students were exposed to Mozart, the Baby Boomers were exposed to the great classics by watching cartoons—specifically the Looney Tunes cartoons. Ingeniously woven into the plots of Elmer Fudd or Daffy Duck cartoons were portions of classical favorites such as Beethoven's *Fifth Symphony* (Da Da Da Dum!), Tchaikovsky's *Nutcracker Suite*, or Rimsky-Korsakov's "Flight of the Bumblebee." Not only were the cartoons entertaining, but music lovers also enjoyed the interweaving of classical favorites. I would love to take a music appreciation class that uses Looney Tunes cartoons to teach the classics!

If music can soothe the savage beast, what benefits can music have on a classroom or entire school of students? What song would you like your students to hear at the beginning of class? Obviously, Brahms's "Lullaby" would not be at the top of your list. I have visited one site that played the Beach Boys' "Be True to Your School" over the sound system before the morning announcements. The kids and teachers were rocking and ready for the day.

You could tailor your daily routine through music. You could play a specific song for each subject about to be taught. Through the use of CDs, it would be simple to locate each song by selecting the track number you want. You could also use specific songs for specific needs throughout the day. For example, you could have an "opening song" to signal the beginning of the day. Aside from the Beach Boys, there are many great choices you can make for this area. You could also play another song to indicate transition time between subjects or time to get ready for lunch or recess. Students will learn these auditory signals quickly.

I often played the Three Tenors while the students were completing "bell work"—work that was available to them on an overhead transparency as they entered the classroom. The students were to enter, put away their things, and work five math problems. When the music stopped, we would go over the math problems, have our verbal overview of the day's agenda, and then begin our day. Stopping the music was our signal. My fifth graders quickly nicknamed the Three Tenors the "Opera Dudes." Only 12-year-olds would think of such a label! They begged for other music choices. We all enjoy variations throughout our days. I would have loved hearing those three melodious voices each morning. The 12-year-olds within my care did not share my love for opera music. Although consistency is wonderful, some students thrive on variation.

Teachers can incorporate music into the learning process by using raps and jingles. Learning multiplication and division facts can be laborious. You can play a CD or tape at the beginning of the day, during cleanup time, or at the end of the day as a supplement. This music can also be used at a learning/listening center or specifically during math time.

Learning the states or capitals is another example of an arduous task for students. I am always amazed that university students (adult learners) can list the names of the United States in alphabetical order. They learned the song "Nifty Fifty United States" as elementary students—and they remember that tune and those lyrics into adulthood.

If students can learn multiplication and division facts or the states in alphabetical order, what other monotonous rote facts can be put to music? The key is the use of "piggyback songs." Basically, the teacher uses a tune that is familiar to all students. One day I asked my adult learners, "How many continents are in the world?" An adult learner stood up and started singing a song to the tune of "Frere Jacques" and pointing to various body parts as she sang (Wolfe, 2001). When she was finished, we all burst into applause—

and laughter. She told us her daughter learned it in kindergarten! Combining song with motions is a great learning tool for students.

While listening to a classical music radio station one day, I discovered that one of my favorite songs as a kid was actually a piggy-back song. Long ago Alan Sherman sang about Camp Granada with the opening lines, "Hello Mudda, Hello Fadda." I learned that the tune is actually "Dance of the Hours" from *La Gioconda* by Amilcare Ponchielli. The composer passed away in 1886—long before Alan Sherman recorded *his* song. Currently, you can hear another version of "Dance of the Hours" from *La Gioconda* in a television commercial in which a golden lab puppy sings the lyrics (the commercial uses some great editing skills) and advertises a tick and flea repellant. I am sure that Ponchielli never dreamed during his lifetime (1834–1886) that this part of his original classical work would be transformed into a song played on the radio and a song used for advertising on digital television. Time will tell the future opportunities that lie in store for Ponchielli's work.

In class I often use "The Twelve Days of Christmas" as our basis for a piggyback song. You can add on to the topic, and it is such fun for the students. After we have the lyrics and tune down, we then attempt to add motions. I am always amused when the adult learners leave class humming the tune.

Language arts teachers can use piggyback songs to teach spelling. Five-letter words can be sung to the tune of "You Are My Sunshine" (Wolfe, 2001). Think of a five-letter word and sing that tune. It really works! According to Wolfe, six-letter words fit the tune of "Happy Birthday to You," and seven-letter words can be sung to "Twinkle, Twinkle, Little Star." Have your class think of other songs that fit words with specific numbers of letters. Older students could do this project in small groups or independently.

Piggyback songs can be about content topics such as nouns or verbs, regrouping in addition or subtraction, or the Lewis and Clark expedition. Piggyback songs are great as a class project, especially when you are introducing this concept. Just select a tune such as "Happy Birthday," "Bingo," or "The Ants Go Marching" and work with the students to write lyrics. Do not restrict your choices to traditional children's songs. One of my adult learners chose the "Theme from the Addams Family" to create a piggyback song based on the topic of the ocean. Every student knew that tune, and we all knew when to snap (snap! snap!) at just the right times. Older students can create piggyback songs independently or in small groups after they understand the mechanics. Use CDs or cassette tapes in a listening center. Teachers working with older students can allow time for them to create piggyback songs to be shared with younger students. Parents transporting students to and from school can also tape-record piggyback songs to be played in the car to promote learning. You can use digital movie cameras to record the students singing piggyback songs and then create a DVD. This would appeal to both the visual and auditory learners. By using rewriteable DVDs, you can continue to add new songs.

Music is a great way to get your point across. I often left singing messages on my son's answering machine. He always returned the calls. "Call your mother" has the same number of syllables as "Hallelujah." I would sing "Call your mother" to the tune of the "Hallelujah" chorus from Handel's *Messiah*. Other great tunes are "La Donna é Mobile" from *Rigoletto* by Verdi, "William Tell Overture" by Rossini, and "Habanera" from *Carmen* by Bizet. Sometimes we see singing telegrams in old movies. This is similar—leaving singing messages on the answering machines, which always get returned.

Music is powerful for students of all ages. Campbell shares the story of Alex in his book *The Mozart Effect for Children: Awakening Your Child's Mind, Health, and Creativity with Music* (2002). According to Campbell, the Russian boy spent the first 6 months in an orphanage before being adopted by an American family. Alex had difficulty relating with other children. When he was 4, the music teacher came into his class ready for a lesson on Eastern European folk songs. She played the lullaby, "Sleep My Little Bird." Alex told the class that it was *his* song. When the teacher played the song again, Alex stood up and swayed in time to the music—as his fellow classmates followed suit. According to Campbell (2002), "Our best guess is that just maybe, his birth mother hummed it to him in utero, or an orphanage caregiver crooned it while rocking him. Something in the tempo, key, and cadence of the lullaby touched a chord deep in Alex's memory, deep in his bones. Something magic" (p. 49).

After reading this excerpt from Campbell, we added more variety to my granddaughter's music immersion program by including Native American flute music and Bob Wills and the Texas Playboys. If Alex related to Eastern European folk songs, my granddaughter will relate Native American music and Texas Swing to her roots! Every region of the country has special music with which they identify. Incorporate that music into your classrooms. I use regional music with my future teachers taking elementary social studies, such as polka and Cajun, and they love it. (And they always tell me that their grandparents still play Bob Wills's music—along with Dr. Wilson.)

Along with regional music, students also benefit from music from different eras. The Big Band sound was part of our culture during the '40s. This was replaced in the '50s by rock and roll. The Beatles were a new form of "British Invasion" in the '60s. The decades continue with various artists and themes that identify each era. As students learn about history, they can be immersed in the music of that day as well. Dust off those Cab Callaway, Benny Goodman, and Tommy Dorsey records and share them with your students.

How can an Eastern European boy connect with a song after 4 years? How can adult learners list the United States in alphabetical order many years, perhaps decades, after learning a song in elementary school? How can students perform better on examinations after hearing the music of Mozart? Music is a powerful tool to be used in the classroom. From firsthand experience, you might want to go light on using opera with fifth graders! Still I think the best closing for this chapter is to go back to the quote from Campbell— music is "something magic"!

- Summary for administrators: Provide your faculty with cassette tape recorders or CD players to use with students each day. Bring in outstanding professional development speakers to share the newest research in the area of music and learning. Play music each morning just prior to the announcements. Yes, the Beach Boys and other great artists will be greatly enjoyed and appreciated by your students and faculty. It will help to set a positive stage for the remainder of the day.

Does your school have a schoolwide reading time? This would be a great time to pipe in classical music over the intercom.

- Summary for teachers: Bring music into your classroom every day as well as throughout the day. Allow the students to create music through the use of piggyback songs. Utilize manufactured tapes and CDs to teach content areas.

  Teach spelling words with the tunes presented in this chapter. This will appeal to the auditory learner. Add movements and the kinesthetic learner is happy as well.

  Take a chance on the Mozart Effect study and play compositions from Mozart prior to testing. You may be surprised at the improvements your students make. I use this technique with my students.

- Summary for community and religious volunteers: Community leaders may wish to play patriotic music. Religious teachers may use various religious music throughout the learning sessions. Remember that your time frame for learning is very limited. Have your selections cued up and ready to play. You can also use music before and after your learning times.

- Summary for homeschool parents: Use your stereo system or cable radio channels to bring in wonderful selections of music to your enriched learning environment. Also play music during work times or test-taking times.

REFERENCES

Burgess, N. (2000). *Excel-ability learning: Music study benefits.* Retrieved April 10, 2006, from www.excel-ability.com/Music/Study/MusBenefits.html.

Campbell, D. (2002). *The Mozart effect for children: Awakening your child's mind, health, and creativity with music.* New York: Quill/Harper Collins Publishers.

Wolfe, P. (2001). *Brain matters: Translating research into classroom practice.* Alexandria, VA: Association for Supervision and Curriculum Development.

10

THE LEARNING
ENVIRONMENT

What do we teach students in school? We teach them that two and two make four and that Paris is the capital of France. When will we also teach them what they are? We should say to each of them: Do you know what you are? You are a marvel! . . . In the millions of years that have passed, there has never been another person like you. You could become a Shakespeare, a Michelangelo, a Beethoven. You have the capacity for anything. Yes, you are a marvel!

—Pablo Casals

The principle goal of education is to create men who are capable of doing new things, not simply of repeating what other generations have done—men who are creative, inventive and discoverers.

—Jean Piaget

This chapter takes a look at the learning environment. There is no specific universal definition of this term. Hopefully, after reading this chapter you will be able to create your own definition. This chapter provides ideas for the classroom teacher, the home-school parent, the parent providing additional help to their children at home, and also the school administrator. This chapter also provides creative ideas for the community volunteer or religious teacher who works with children for a short period of time each day or week.

The most important element of the learning environment is enrichment. Again, this term has no universal definition either. Our ultimate goal is to provide an enriched learning environment for children—learning either at home or at school or both.

One summer my family was blessed to have a new cat visit. Soon we discovered that the new cat would be having kittens. I was thrilled because I had not had kittens to play with since the summer that Neil Armstrong walked on the moon. My husband, on the other hand, was far from thrilled. As time passed, we were blessed with three kittens. I have been reading about an enriched learning environment, so I decided to try out some of my ideas on the kittens. I would give them a different "learning environment" each day by placing them on a different carpet sample or a different towel. I did not conduct a pre- or posttest on those kittens, but I am convinced that they were above average in intelligence. We cannot measure the effects of various visual stimuli on kittens—yet—but as educators we can attempt to provide the best learning environment possible for our students.

An underlying factor in this enriched learning environment is safety. We need to take a look at this topic from various aspects to be sure that this great idea you read in a book will be safe in the learning environment you are attempting to create and enrich. A second underlying factor is distractibility. Every group of students is unique. Every child is unique. Do not create enriched environment overkill. Too many stimuli will lead to distractions so that the students cannot focus on the learning opportunity at hand.

When creating an enriched learning environment, consider the contents of the previous chapters. Research has proven that students benefit from increased oxygen, increased intake of fluids or water, nutrition throughout the day, increased movement or exercise, and the use of color when learning. We also recall from previous chapters that we all learn in three basic ways—auditory, visual, or kinesthetic. These are the basic building blocks to consider when creating an enriched learning environment for children. These elements will also provide the teacher with students who are at their optimal level for learning. Wouldn't it be great to teach students who are primed and ready for learning?

MATERIALS FOR A LEARNING ENVIRONMENT

The list of materials needed to create an enriched learning environment varies depending on the age group of the students. There are, however, many standard materials needed to promote optimal learning. These materials go beyond the basics of water, oxygen, and other essentials previously mentioned. Keep a running list of classroom supplies so you will have the list ready when school begins. This list will include materials that will promote learning for the auditory, visual, and kinesthetic learners. You can also ask for donations throughout the year. If you are teaching as a community volunteer or religious trainer, go to the parents or caregivers of your students for supplies. It has long been up to the teacher to provide supplies for students. Break that financial cycle and ask for supplies from other sources. Parents and caregivers will be happy to help out when they are aware of specific items that are needed.

New products are always making an entrance into the consumer market. Recently we have seen the introduction of colored permanent markers. This allows teachers and students to use a variety of colors on plastic and synthetic materials that were once reserved for black. Along with colored permanent markers we now have washable glue and washable crayons. This is wonderful for cleanup—both of the learning environment and also of the students! Glittered glue is a fun option for children. This is a wonderful alternative to the standard wet glue covered with glitter—which eventually gets all over the learning environment and the children.

Clay has also had major improvements over the years. Children need this type of medium to build 3-D forms, just as they need the previously mentioned items to create dazzling art creations. Pipe cleaners of various colors and sizes are also great for 3-D works of art.

Please select the type of scissors that is age appropriate. The younger children need the scissors with rounded tips. The older students enjoy working with the sharp pointed scissors. Remember the "lefties" and try to keep a few pairs of left-handed scissors in the classroom. Farris (2004) suggests that 5-year-olds use paper that is at least 11 inches by 14 inches. "Five-year-olds practice using pencils, pens, markers, and crayons. . . . A variety of writing instruments and kinds of paper are desirable so that children can learn the physical limitations of each kind" (p. 304).

Consider establishing a scrap box to recycle colored paper. This can be any type of container with or without a lid. Place it in a location where it can be easily accessed and, most importantly, used. Virtually any size or shape of paper can be added to the scrap box, and the more colorful the better.

Depending on the age of the students, consider items for a "store." Save used boxes and containers that can become items or stock for the store. Other items for students could include used margarine tubs. These can be used for storage, or students can use the tubs or covers to trace circles.

Along with pretending to run a store, children enjoy playing with puppets. They provide children a way to develop their oral expression. Children develop language in four basic stages—listening, speaking, reading, and writing. Although they may not yet have developed reading and writing skills, they still have good listening and speaking skills awaiting creative uses. Puppets do not need to be the expensive store-bought variety. They can be as easy as a sock (used or new) with marker faces. This type of puppet really stretches the imagination! Children can help make their own puppets. Need a stage? Put a cloth over a desk, and you are good to go.

Consider the purpose of your classroom. If you are teaching mathematics skills, include basic sorting and grouping materials such as various macaroni shapes, assorted buttons, a choice of types of dried beans, and used sewing spools. You can think of other household items that would be age appropriate manipulatives for children.

Children also need visual stimulation—books and printed materials. According to Farris (2004),

> A well-stocked book corner is an asset to any early childhood classroom. It should include a wide variety of books, including mail-order catalogs, a first encyclopedia, phone books, nursery rhymes, fairy tales, big books (both commercially published and those made in class), modern books, traditional fables, poetry, children's magazines (such as *Lady bug, Spider, Appleseed,* and *Our Big Outdoors*), brochures, music, and maps. (p. 302)

Most importantly, Farris (2004) recommends that "the books should also reflect the diversity within the classroom and the community so that children see themselves represented in these stories" (p. 302). Farris recommends "six books for each child in the class and to change the books every three weeks" (p. 302).

THE GEOGRAPHY OF THE LEARNING ENVIRONMENT

In social studies classes, we look at longitude and latitude when teaching geography. If we take that concept and apply it to teaching, we are providing learning opportunities at various heights and spans in the learning environment.

Can you put learning opportunities on the ceiling? Yes, if it is within the fire code for your learning environment. The ceiling is often an overlooked space to provide great visuals for children. My dentist has the ceiling decorated, and I see it when I am in the dentist's chair. Why not utilize the ceiling for your students? I would love to visit a classroom where the teacher refers the students to the chart on the ceiling above the doorway. This would provide daydreamers who gaze at the ceiling with great opportunities to learn.

Also consider the floor. Part of my job with the university is to supervise teachers during their first year. Because I have numerous teaching certifications, I have had the opportunity to work with over 40 first-year teachers at various curriculum and grade levels. I think we can all learn from early childhood teachers. Many early childhood teachers sit on the floor and teach at eye level. Each time I observe lessons in this fashion, I am always amazed at how engaged the students are in the lessons. It's tough to misbehave when you are sitting next to your teachers—at the same level. The teacher can see any potential problem and nip it in the bud before it occurs—a proactive approach to classroom discipline. This concept of teaching at eye level corresponds with the idea of locking holes. The teacher is right at eye level—or close to that—and has the ultimate attention of the students. The teacher has direct eye contact with students. When you work with older children, this approach may not be feasible for whole-class instruction. It can, however, be utilized during small-group instruction such as reading groups or math groups.

Compare this approach to the usual teaching position of standing and circulating around the classroom. Children may feel intimidated with the teacher so high above them. They are looking up at the teacher throughout the day.

The issue of latitude/longitude in instruction also arises when using visuals. When you use overhead transparencies, be sure that they are high enough for students sitting at the back to see over others' heads. This needs to be set at a reasonable height for everyone.

Because we are incorporating not only visuals but also auditory stimulation with our lessons, take a look around the room for a good spot for your CD player or auditory source. This spot needs to be centralized so that everyone can hear well, and it also needs to be close to an electrical outlet. If you are going to leave the player plugged in each day, you may need to tape down the cord so that no student or teacher trips over the cord. Student safety is paramount.

Classroom teachers are geniuses in arranging bulletin boards, word walls, and other learning opportunities around the room, ceiling, and floor. When you consider the geography of the learning environment, are there any overlooked spaces in your environment that you can use well? A few years ago, a friend sent me an e-mail about using magnetic paint for learning opportunities. I copied the message and passed it out to my students. Over time, these students have become classroom teachers who have used magnetic paint in a special location in their classrooms.

The most unique space utilized for this learning opportunity was the space *below* the chalkboard or whiteboard. I had never heard of anyone ever using this space. She provided inexpensive magnetic letters and numbers for the children as they sat on the floor and used the special space. She also took 1-inch tiles (the ones that are connected that go in showers) that were donated from a carpet and tile store and wrote consonant blends, prefixes and suffixes, and math functions ($+ - \times / =$). She then attached magnetic tape to the back of each tile. (Another tip is to cut apart children's place-mats and attach the magnetic tape to the back of each piece. They are affordable, can be used a zillion times, and can be cleaned with antibacterial wipes to prevent sharing germs. These can be kept in resealable bags.) Rather than painting the space black to match the chalkboard, she painted it *hot pink*! She had listened to too many of my lectures on the learning benefits of utilizing color, and she put the theory into practice.

If you choose to take on a project similar to this, please check with your administrator during the planning phase. He or she may be able to find funds to pay for the project. Your administrator will have a definite point of view about painting a section of your classroom wall with magnetic paint. Do advance research on initial cost prior to your visit. Read the directions in advance and follow them closely. I have been told by my teaching friends who have done this project that you will use *several* paint sponge brushes in this process. That element needs to be added to your cost. Most importantly, do not select a space that is too high for your children to use. If you have physically disabled students using wheelchairs, the space needs to be accessible to them as well. Keep the longitude and latitude of learning in mind. Tip: When you are giving your pitch to the administrator regarding cost-effectiveness, point out that this project will be used by students not only this year, but in future years as well. This is a perpetual pro-ject that will be used by students for many years to come.

This section started with learning opportunities on the ceiling and progressed to various areas of the classroom. Einstein said, "Creativity is more important than intelligence." Think creatively when designing learning opportunities for your students.

WORD WALLS

The purpose of a word wall is to provide learners with constant visual stimulation of words that they can spell or read. As their reading and writing abilities improve, the word wall grows. You can utilize color and also visuals with word walls to enhance learning even more. Word walls can be set up in classrooms, children's bedrooms, or a room used by a community volunteer or religious teacher. They are as versatile as the children they are intended to serve.

Word walls can continuously grow, or they can be set up in advance. Another idea for a word wall is to create it for a specific theme or season such as back to school or autumn. As the theme or season changes, a new word wall appears. Word walls can be as versatile or as consistent as you wish.

Word walls are an essential part of an enriched learning environment. Referring back to the previous section on the geography of the learning environment, take a long look at your classroom and decide on the best location for your word wall. No space? You can find space. Remember, there is always the ceiling. Some classroom teachers attach information to the curtains. Some use the space *above* the whiteboard or chalkboard.

At the beginning of school in first grade, the word wall is very small. A great idea is to include the first names of students in the classroom on the word wall. Other students will learn how to spell their names. If you are creating a word wall for home use, consider including the names of family members—along with pictures beside each name.

Also consider including a picture or photo, if possible, with the words. I visited the home of a family friend with a special needs child. The parents and older sibling had worked together to create a word wall on the child's bedroom wall. To help promote learning, they had included colored pictures from magazines or clip art to place beside the nouns. Obviously, this would appeal to the visual learner. I believe that *all* children can benefit from this additional attention to visual detail.

Create a kinesthetic word wall by using darker background paper and alphabet cereal. Most cereals are light tan-colored and need a strong background color to create good contrast. The child can actually feel the words. They could take the slips of paper off the word wall and create word rubbings. This type of word wall would appeal to kinesthetic learners when they help to create it or when they feel it. It would also be helpful to special needs students who are visually impaired.

In the previous section, magnetic paint was discussed. A magnetic section on a wall could be the focal point for a word wall in a classroom, a room at home, or room in a community center or religious teaching room. You could attach magnetic tape to each section of paper. This would work well if you had each section laminated also. Colored markers or colored background paper would enhance learning. You could also use the computer to make letters large or colored. I often cut up old file folders for all types of projects. Gently used file folders would work well as part of a magnetic word wall. When using a magnetic learning area in any setting, remember to paint it low enough for *all* students to best utilize it.

A final word wall suggestion is to set it up on student paper and keep it in the child's notebook—a *word page* rather than a word wall. This could be done by allowing the students to write their own words for the "wall" or page. The teacher or parent could also create this using a word processor program on the computer. This could be saved and reused each year.

You could set up word pages that use themes or seasons also. The child would then have several pages as reference rather than just one. The student could create visuals by drawing pictures of the nouns.

SHOWER CURTAINS

Shower curtains are inexpensive canvases for learning opportunities that incorporate multiple learning styles. Shower curtains can become giant colorful game boards on the floor. Children can crawl on the curtain while playing the games. Shower curtains can also be folded flat and easily stored.

You can place shower curtains on the wall for a huge learning opportunity. You could trace maps onto shower curtains using an overhead projector and permanent markers. (Remember that permanent markers come in a variety of colors now.) This would be a good Plan B if you do not have current maps in your classroom.

Aside from creating learning opportunities on the shower curtains, you can find inexpensive curtains that have learning opportunities already designed on them. I bought a world map shower curtain for my son when he was in elementary school. He was saturated with learning opportunities every time he took a shower. We would also go to the shower to check the curtain if we ever had a geography question. It was a great resource.

STORAGE

A question that I am frequently asked by home school parents is "Where do we store everything?" This is a good question for classroom teachers, religious teachers and community volunteers, parents helping their children learn at home, and administrators—and university professors.

- Resealable bags come in a variety of sizes. They are fantastic. Classroom teachers: consider including these as part of your school supply list at the beginning of school. Other readers: stock up when they go on sale.
- Space bags are much newer to the market. They will not solve all space problems, but they work very well for some items. You could store a zillion shower curtains in one space bag.
- Pizza boxes are great to store great learning opportunities as well as student-generated work. I keep my portfolio in digital form as well as in hard copy form. If I were 7, I would keep the hard copy in a pizza box. Pizza boxes come in a variety of sizes. You can ask your neighborhood pizza parlor for donations.

To create a pizza box portfolio, allow the students to decorate their own boxes. They need to write their names on the *side* of the box rather than the top of the box. The boxes can then be stacked on top of each other, and you can read the name on the side of the box. Student and teacher "choices" can be added to the portfolio throughout the year. At the end of the school year, the portfolio is ready to go home. If children transfer during the school year, they can take the portfolios when they leave. This is a great idea and basically free to the school. Religious teachers or community volunteers could also store student work in pizza boxes and send them home at regular intervals.

CREATING AN ENVIRONMENT WITH GOOD TRAFFIC FLOW

I visit many different classrooms each year. As I travel to the designated classrooms, I always take a look inside other classrooms along the way. Many classrooms are designed for free accessibility to all learning areas within the classroom. These classrooms provide easy movement for the students and teacher.

Other classrooms are less congenially arranged. The best bad example that I have is the classroom in which the pencil sharpener was *behind* the file cabinet. Apparently the file cabinet was moved in front of the pencil sharpener. After the teacher's attention was drawn to this, the file cabinet was moved to another location.

Take a long look at your learning environment. Can the children get to every nook and cranny easily? If not, take a look at other classrooms at your school site. You can emulate those room arrangements to meet the needs of your students and your classroom.

Where is the front of your classroom? The students need to be able to see the day's agenda and the visuals you will be showing during instruction. Can every student easily come to the front of the room to write on the whiteboards or chalkboards?

You can elect to place the student desks in pods or quads. (*Quad* means four students per group.) You can arrange the entire class in a

U shape. You can "circle the wagons" by placing the desks in a semi-circle or an entire circle shape. The arrangement of the student desks is up to you, but consider where the front of the room is located. Also consider where you will post your classroom rules. If the students are facing numerous directions, place the rules on *every* wall. This will accommodate all children, no matter where they are sitting. Rather than printing your rules on one sheet of paper using size 12 font, consider printing each rule on a single sheet of paper (using a large font) and posting the rules on every wall. This will provide continuous visual reinforcement to every student throughout the day.

STATING EXPECTATIONS

If you are working with 2-year-olds or 102-year-olds, let the students know what your expectations are for the lesson or time frame. For a short time I taught the 2- and 3-year-old Sunday school class. Some people thought it was a waste for a university professor to be working with such small minds. I never worked so hard—for free. I learned tons from those little tikes!

I decided to sit them down at the beginning of each morning and tell them exactly what we were going to do. We would pray, learn about _____, pray again, and then have the option of doing X or Y. They listened to my opening remarks—and remembered them. I could not make any changes to the agenda or they would call me on it. Because they knew exactly what was going to happen, they thrived on the structure. It was also a good approach to take when I worked with children for a very short time frame. I always had the option of changing the routine for next week.

This stating of expectations can be used by homeschool parents and community volunteers. Administrators can use this technique at the beginning of faculty meetings. Classroom teachers can state their expectations for each lesson, then review those expectations during the conclusion of the lesson. The students will be excited about getting a preview of the wonderful learning opportunities they have waiting for them.

- Summary for administrators: As teachers attempt to provide an enriched learning environment for their students, work with the teachers to have supplies readily available. If they need colored markers or shower curtains—items that may not necessarily be on the regular supply list—work with them to find the resources to buy these materials. As these super creative educators attempt to utilize every possible inch of the learning environment, check with the fire marshal about specific fire codes that apply to your school site—and inform the teachers of these restrictions.
- Work with your teachers in all aspects of safety. Encourage them to tape down electrical cords. Encourage them to use fire retardant fabrics.

Provide a networking system in which you share creative ideas with other teachers through the daily/weekly communication system. You can also share ideas within and among other administrators in your district. Take digital photos and include them along with a narrative text. A flaw of many educators is the absence of networking, in which they have no idea what is going on in the rooms across or down the hall, let alone what great things are going on in other buildings. The administrator can become the networking agent for teachers within the district.

Work with nearby businesses to coordinate a school donation drive. Allow area businesses to donate needed supplies—those that will help to provide an enriched learning environment for auditory, visual, and kinesthetic learners. Compile a well-designed list of necessary items that may not necessarily be considered standard school supplies. Ask businesses to post the list on their lounge bulletin boards. Employees who do not have children in school may be interested in helping provide supplies to teachers.

Create posters to be displayed in the businesses. This information will get out to many school patrons who might not know that such items are needed for the school.

Along with the flyers or posters, ask the businesses if you can place a donation box in their location. Designate someone to visit the donation box on a regular basis. If you don't check often and regularly, donors will become hesitant to give in the future.

After you have prepared your requests and received them, how will you thank the patrons? Consider allowing students to write or create thank you letters or notes to be sent to the locations in which you receive donations. Yes, a letter on school stationary is a wonderful way to thank individuals, but a child-created note or letter will warm the hearts of the benevolent donors.

Finally, work with the faculty to provide an enriched learning environment for the students. Invite innovative speakers to provide staff development workshops for your faculty. Purchase creative DVDs or VHS tapes for faculty members to review during more convenient times. Work with the professional development coordinators at the district level to bring in the best possible opportunities for the faculty—or to send the faculty to those opportunities.

- Summary for teachers: The suggestions in this chapter will appeal to all learning styles as well as appeal to students with special learning needs. These suggestions will help to promote long-term learning.

Examine every inch of your classroom to find unused spaces that you can develop into wonderful learning opportunities for your students. Yes, consider the ceiling.

Use color and visuals with your word wall. Set it up to appeal to the learning levels of your students. Consider the cost-effectiveness of establishing a magnetic learning area.

Work with other teachers at your grade level or subject area to design a list of supplies that may be donated from sources other than parents. Make these requests known to your administrator.

Consider the geography of learning when setting up or rearranging your classroom. Get down to the students' level, lock holes for some lessons.

Have fun with that word wall. Create a visual or kinesthetic wall. Make it as colorful as possible. Remember to add "Dr. Wilson" to your wall! Or have the students design word pages complete with student-created visuals.

Bring in pizza boxes for the children to personally design to store their work. Select a good location—an organization station—for these boxes.

Tell your students exactly what they will be doing during the lesson. Then restate that again during your conclusion. Share your expectations with the students.

- Summary for homeschool parents: This chapter offers a zillion ways for parents to create an enriched learning environment. You can set this up in a single room or place stations throughout your home.

  Interesting materials have been suggested in this chapter. You can pull socks from a drawer or beans from the kitchen cabinet to provide learning opportunities.

  Set up the word wall to last the year or just for a single season or holiday. You establish the way you want to utilize word walls.

  You may choose to help your children create word pages rather than walls. This chapter provides information to help. These can be hand written or computer generated.

  No space for storage? The chapter includes a variety of suggestions for storage of special papers and projects.

  When you replace the shower curtain, consider purchasing one that will provide continuous learning opportunities for those showering. Also purchase an inexpensive plain curtain that you and your children can design into a marvelous learning opportunity or game.

  You have the luxury of teaching at eye level. You can easily read your child's work as he or she completes it. Still, remember the geography of your learning environment. Provide some variety in instruction—both for you and for your students.

- Summary for community and religious volunteers: I hope this chapter has been a valuable tool for you. When I was purchasing back-to-school items this fall, I found out that our Sunday school classes were short on basic supplies. I gave to them rather than to the schools. You need to be continually taking inventory of needed supplies and communicate these needs to your supervisors. Also think outside the box when requesting supplies. Rather than the basic paper, pencils, glue, scissors, and crayons, what other unique manipulatives would benefit your students?

Set up your learning environment so that it is appealing to little eyes. Be aware of the flow of traffic and the seating arrangement. Where is the front of your room? You may or may not need a front.

Tell the students your expectations for the day. Give them a short introduction and conclude the day's task with a summary. Students of all ages benefit from that format.

REFERENCE

Farris, P. (2004). *Elementary and middle school social studies: An interdisciplinary, multicultural approach* (4th ed.). Boston: McGraw-Hill.

III

ESSENTIALS FOR THE LEARNING ENVIORNMENT

11

MANAGING/LEADING THE LEARNING ENVIRONMENT

It is the supreme art of the teacher to awaken joy in creative expression and knowledge.

—Albert Einstein

Many universities offer a course entitled Classroom Management. This is a marvelous course for future teachers. One of my students referred to the course as the "meat and potatoes" of his degree plan. The question arises, "Exactly *what* are you managing?" This chapter discusses the topics you will be managing and also leading.

You can recall various occupations that relate directly to management. What do those individuals manage? Probably widgets and various items like that. As the educational manager and leader of your enriched learning environment, what is there for you to manage? You will be in charge of identifying locations for learning centers, designing arrangements for student desks, and defining special curricular areas such as listening centers or reading rug areas. You will design a classroom that has good traffic flow. You will create a safe learning environment in which the electrical cords are taped down to the floor to prevent anyone tripping over them. You will manage the widgets of your classroom.

You can also recall various occupations that require leadership. Obviously, the military is seeking individuals with good leadership skills. That's because the military is leading *people*. Douglas MacArthur and

George Patton were leaders. Education is also looking for individuals with good leadership skills—classroom leadership. You will be the educational leader in your enriched learning environment. You will lead your students. If you think you are going to manage them, reconsider that thought. You are not going to *manage* children. Over time, you will develop a repertoire of various leadership techniques that will be successful with your students.

The previous chapter discussed stating your expectations. This chapter discusses teaching rules in your classroom or enriched learning environment. A rule is something that can be measured. That is a paramount statement. Rather than a suggestion such as "please smile" or "always cheer for others" or "share," a rule is a behavior that you specifically do or do not want to occur. Are you willing to call parents or send a child to the principal's office if they break a rule? Yes! Classrooms have rules. The cafeteria has rules. The playground has rules. Arriving and departing from school involves rules. These are desirable behaviors that help to provide security, safety, and uninterrupted learning.

I once observed a lesson that was the very first time the students ever worked in groups. They had absolutely no idea how to behave. They were all over the place, visiting with everyone in the class, doing everything except the assigned task. Following the lesson, I discussed things with the teacher. She had not discussed her expectations for behaviors during group work with the students—yet she chose this type of lesson when the university representative came to visit. She *did* have that discussion immediately after I pulled out of the parking lot. Please establish rules for working in groups.

How do you want the students to behave during group work? Work with your students to establish these rules, and then take time to teach the students the rules over the span of several days. Below are some suggestions for rules for group work.

Possible Rules for Group Work

- Please speak only to your group members.
- Stay in your seat.

- Every member of the group helps to clean up.
- Remember your time limit.

Some teachers have special circumstances in their classroom that require special rules. The music teacher requires special rules for handling musical instruments or keeping sheet music in order. The computer teacher has rules for using the computers properly. He or she may also have a limit on the number of pages students can print. The gym or PE teacher has rules for proper use of the equipment. Many libraries have a limit on the number of books that can be checked out.

YOUR CLASSROOM RULES

I am in and out of school and classrooms each week. I enjoy peeking into classrooms to see the room setup, the rules, and any special centers that the teacher has created. Often I see beautiful, colorful classroom rules—that were purchased. Apparently a company halfway across the country decided what rules teachers would have and put them into a colorful design—and the teachers bought it. You need to create rules that specifically meet the needs of your students and the enriched learning environment that you created. Take ownership of this important task. If the chart is colorful and beautiful, it is because you designed it that way, not a company 500 miles away.

When you set up classroom rules for your enriched learning environment, what behaviors are of paramount importance to you? What behaviors do you want to avoid? I am always making school visits and looking inside classrooms. I have seen some very poor excuses for classroom rules. (To refresh your memory, rules promote desired behaviors that help to provide security, safety, and uninterrupted learning. Rules are *measurable*. Rules are taught and retaught to your students many times until they become part of the fabric of your classroom.)

The word *respect* or *respectful* is part of many rules that I observe on classroom walls. How can you measure if a student is showing respect or is behaving in a respectful manner? Remember, you should be willing to call parents or send the child to the principal's office if he or she breaks rules. Because respect is so subject to interpretation, it should be eliminated from the list of rules. One individual's version of respect may not necessarily be the same as another individual's. How will you feel when you send a student to the principal's office and he or she tells the principal that he or she *was* being respectful? Select rules that do not leave room for debate. Establish rules that are measurable and objective.

When writing your rules, write them in a positive manner. As I entered one school, posted on the outside door was a page of information telling me what *not* to do. I had just arrived and had not had time to commit any of these infractions. Neither had any of the other visitors using this entrance. I did not appreciate the negativity—neither did the other individuals using that entrance. Avoid negative statements and using the words "do not."

KEEP THE NUMBER OF RULES TO FIVE OR FEWER

When working with children, keep the number of rules down to a minimum. When working with children in a community or religious setting, keep the number of rules to a minimum. I once worked with a high school teacher who had 28 different classroom rules. Neither the teacher nor the students could ever keep track of the rules! Establish the basic rules that you believe are paramount—and keep the number of rules down.

CLASSROOM TEACHERS: NUMBER YOUR RULES

When you have a small number of rules, you can assign a specific number to each rule. You then record the infraction along with the child's name in your plan book each day. At times, a pattern can form showing the same misbehaviors occurring over time. You may even see the pattern occurring the same day each week. A parent conference can shed light on the source of these patterns.

Mr. White's Classroom Rules

1. Bring your supplies, book, assignments, and pencils to class each day.
2. Assignments are due at the beginning of class each day.

You may wish to break the rules down even more specifically. A suggestion follows.

Mr. Black's Classroom Rules

1. Bring your supplies each day.
2. Bring your books each day.
3. Bring your assignments each day.
4. Bring your pencils each day.
5. Assignments are due at the beginning of class each day.

The additional documentation can also help the classroom teacher to establish and maintain credibility with colleagues, the administration, and parents. Rather than trying to think of the day or week that an infraction occurred, you have accessible data quickly and readily available.

CREATE MEASURABLE, OBJECTIVE RULES

When you brainstorm about possible rules for your classroom, restrict your options to only measurable rules. We would love for everyone to be honest, truthful, and respectful. These behaviors cannot be measured. Rather than assigning these traits as rules—and putting yourself in potentially bad situations with parents and administrators—choose, instead, measurable, objective rules.

What behaviors do you want? Do you want them to bring their pencils, assignments, books, and supplies each day? Then write that down as Rule 1. That rule is measurable. If someone comes unprepared, write his or her name down in the grade book or plan book along with the rule number.

Once your rules are established, take time to teach them over several days until they are learned. Then revisit them, perhaps weekly, to reinforce them with the students. We all need refresher courses. Also post your classroom rules on all four walls. Put each rule on a single sheet of paper and make the font size large. I suggest putting them on colored paper or using a large colored font. You will be the only teacher at your school site that makes the extra effort to display your rules in this manner—and your colleagues and administrators will notice.

Once you have established your classroom rules, then what? Sit down with your administrator or send him or her a copy for approval. Then send a letter home to parents along with the list of rules. Some teachers will create a sign-and-return request at the bottom of the page. If they sign and return the page, how will they be able to keep the list of rules? Design a communication that allows them to keep the rules and return a slip to you to verify that they have received them.

EXPLAIN WHY WE NEED THESE RULES

Be prepared for the ultimate question asked by students on a minute-by-minute basis, "Why?" Someone will inevitably ask you *why* we have a certain rule. Of course, the obvious response is, "Because I am the teacher!" But seriously, teach the rationale when you teach the rules. Embrace this teachable moment. When the students understand the paramount importance, they will more likely comply. Remember, you have five or fewer rules. These are of the highest importance and in the best interest of the class. Tell them why.

I taught at a school site that housed every physically handicapped and disabled elementary student in the district. We had children who wore leg braces. We had children confined to wheelchairs. We had children who used crutches. My fifth graders *knew* why they could never, ever run in the hallways: They could get hurt or they could hurt someone else. We had the largest bodies in the school. We could run the fastest. If we ran, bad things could happen. If they weren't concerned about hurting someone else, I always got their attention when I told them that *they* could be hurt. The egocentric ones always listened to that particular portion of my speech. Running in the halls is never condoned, but at our particular school site the prohibition was necessary for human safety reasons. Because I took the time to explain (over and over) *why* they could not run, they complied.

You have specific rationales for each rule that you have selected. Take the time to explain the reasons to your students. It will help them internalize the reasons. (Toss in "Don't run in the hallways" just once for me!)

WHAT ARE PROCEDURES?

Many teachers also have procedures. These are general directions that help us get through our day. Many teachers ask children to have their pencils sharpened before class begins—it never happens, but they often ask children to comply. This would be a procedure. Other procedures could include expected actions during tornado, earthquake, fire drill, or school lockdown procedures. Teachers need to be prepared, and the students need to know what to do. A general classroom example would be to have only one person at the pencil sharpener at a time. Again, it never happens, but they often request it. Sometimes teachers will leap into proactive mode and inspect the pencils before they are sharpened. I hope you have better ways to spend your time!

You may have procedures for transition time—moving from one lesson to another or from one classroom to another. You might have procedures for using centers, such as the listening center or the science center. Many teachers have procedures for using the classroom computer. These are all great ideas. These procedures are taught verbally. Rarely are procedures written down. As with classroom rules, please take time to teach your procedures for several days, then revisit them weekly for a quick review.

CONSEQUENCES AND REWARDS/INCENTIVES

Along with establishing classroom rules, the classroom teacher needs to set reasonable consequences for the students. Just as you teach the rules for several days and then review them weekly, you need to do the same with the consequences. The easiest consequence on the planet is "miss X number of minutes of recess." Before establishing that as a consequence, revisit the information in chapter 7. There really *are* benefits to movement and exercise. I thought it was so important that I made it a special chapter in this book! Perhaps the child would benefit much more from getting outside, running, jumping, yelling, screaming, and getting fresh air. Think outside the box. Get feedback from other teachers and your administrator. Design a set of consequences that works for your students—and you.

I often laugh at the grocery store when I hear a highly frustrated parent ask a child, "Do you want a spanking?" I have yet to hear a child respond affirmatively to that question. Sometimes teachers, as well as parents, paint themselves into a corner. I've heard teachers tell a student, "Don't make me come back there!" I wonder why they aren't monitoring the classroom by moving to all locations. Some teachers will ask, "Do you want to go to the principal's office?" When you have established a set of consequences, you don't get painted into a corner. You are prepared—proactively—to tackle misbehaviors and problems that occur.

Just as with the classroom rules, you want to make your administrator and parents/caregivers aware of your consequences. Provide this information at the beginning of the school year or when you take over as the educational leader of your enriched learning environment.

Just as you have consequences, you need to have rewards or incentives for your students. You can set this up for individuals, the class, or both. I have seen situations in which the classroom teacher is so busy rewarding each student through the day that he or she barely has time to teach. Establish a system that is a win-win situation for everyone.

When deciding on an incentive to use with students, select one that is low cost or no cost to you. Because you will be working on more than one incentive program throughout the year, the tab will mount if you are paying for everything.

I taught before VCRs were invented. The teachers in my day had to think outside the box for a classwide incentive—that was cheap or free. We came up with class baseball games or foursquare or hopscotch tournaments. Once during the winter months, I had a jacks tournament. (The kids thought it was a new game!) Because we didn't do this as an entire class event every day, the students had high anticipation about the experience.

Sometimes you need to plan for a class incentive or reward that can be pulled off regardless of the weather. My nephew was thrilled one winter to participate in a class "beach party." He brought his beach towel to school along with some snacks. They rearranged the chairs and desks and partied in the classroom.

One final contemplation: Consider what will happen to the reward or incentive program when you are away from school. Do you want a substitute to pass out treats or certificates? Explain your wishes in writing in your substitute folder.

FOR HOMESCHOOL PARENTS

What rules do you need your children to follow every time you sit down to teach them? If you choose to establish a small set of five or fewer rules for your enriched learning environment, please follow the steps given in this chapter.

As a parent, you already have told your children what to do in case of an emergency. You might involve them, as part of a learning opportunity, in revamping those procedures. Where is your family supposed to gather in case of a tornado? What do you need to create a tornado kit to be ready? The great educator of the early 20th century, John Dewey, wrote and taught often about "teachable moments." Take this opportunity—this teachable moment—to involve your children in this family project.

The same is true for planning what to do if you have a fire in the house—or if you live in an area that has grass fires that would get close to your home. Involve your children in developing a plan of action for the family—including the pets. What items would you need to grab as you evacuated, and why would you take *those* items?

FOR THE COMMUNITY VOLUNTEER OR RELIGIOUS TEACHER

I realize that you may see your students for only a limited amount of time each week. You may not even have a classroom. Rather than rules and procedures, consider specific safety needs that you need to address with the children. Follow the methods stated above about teaching, reteaching, and continuously reviewing the group needs.

I served on a committee at church that designed safety rules for our church site. I suggested that we post the safety procedures in each Sunday school classroom. Because people were using those rooms only once weekly, they could forget what to do in case of a fire or tornado. We also had substitutes who helped out only once who were not familiar at all with the procedures. Visual reminders needed to be posted for all to see. You might use this approach in your location. Just stick to the basic safety needs of the children.

PUTTING IT ALL TOGETHER

What is the secret to becoming an effective leader or manager of your enriched learning environment? The research team of Emmer, Evertson, and Anderson (as cited in Borish, 2000) took a look at this very topic. They concluded that effective teachers (leaders and managers)

> established themselves as instructional leaders early in the school year. They worked on rules and procedures until students learned them. Instructional content was important for these teachers, but they also stressed group cohesiveness and socialization, achieving a

common set of classroom norms. By the end of the first three weeks, they were ready for the rest of the year. (p. 378)

You can follow the findings of these researchers. You can come to teach each day, beginning with day 1. You can have those rules and procedures prepared before the children walk into the room. You then teach them and reteach them until the content is learned—according to Emmer, Evertson, and Anderson this may take the first 3 weeks of school. Then revisit those procedures and rules weekly for a quick review. Just as you teach and reteach the rules and procedures, you will do the same with the consequences and rewards or incentives. Keep the students informed about your expectations for their behavior.

- Summary for administrators: Work with the central office to stay current on safety procedures for your staff and faculty. Have frequent drills so that everyone—including the students—know the procedure.

  Work with the first-year teachers prior to the beginning of school to be sure they have measurable rules ready to go. Encourage them to post them on all four walls of their classrooms. Request a copy of the letter that will go home to explain the rules, consequences, and rewards. You can use those copies as great examples for the next year's group of first-year teachers.

  Provide professional development materials and seminars for faculty on the various models of discipline or management. Burden (2006) divides the models into three groups—low teacher control approaches, medium teacher control approaches, and high teacher control approaches. The grouping by Burden is as follows:

Low Teacher Control Approaches

Congruent Communication: Haim Ginott
Discipline as Self-Control: Thomas Gordon
Teaching with Love and Logic: Jim Fay and David Funk
Inner Discipline: Barbara Coloroso
From Discipline to Community: Alfie Kohn

Medium Teacher Control Approaches

Logical Consequences: Rudolf Dreikurs
Cooperative Discipline: Linda Albert
Positive Discipline: Jane Nelsen, Lynn Lott, and H. Stephen Glenn
Noncoercive Discipline: William Glasser
Discipline with Dignity: Richard Curwin and Allen Mendler
Win-Win Discipline: Spencer Kagan

High Teacher Control Approaches

Behavior Modification: B. F. Skinner
Assertive Discipline: Lee and Marlene Canter
Positive Discipline: Frederic Jones (p. 16)

- Summary for teachers: Remember the five-or-fewer approach to establishing measurable rules for your classroom. Use creative consequences and incentives. Work with your administrator and parents to be sure everyone is aware of the policy.

  Teach and reteach until the students know the information. Then revisit the policies at least once each week. Your attention to this process will pay off in huge dividends over the course of the school year.
- Summary for homeschool parents: Establish guidelines for your enriched learning environment and be consistent to stay with those guidelines.
- Summary for community and religious volunteers: Be aware of the safety and security procedures at your site. Take time to teach this information to the children.

REFERENCES

Burden, P. (2006). *Classroom management: Creating a successful K–12 learning community* (3rd ed.). Hoboken, NJ: Wiley Jossey-Bass Education.

COMMUNICATION SKILLS FOR AN ENRICHED LEARNING ENVIRONMENT

Education is not preparation for life; education is life itself.

—John Dewey

You have planned, you have prepared, you are ready to provide long-term learning[2] for your students. You have explained your expectations to your class. Is there anyone else you need to communicate with? *Yes!* You need to communicate with the children's parents, with your administrator, and with your colleagues.

Hillary Clinton wrote a book that explains that it takes a village to raise a child. It takes a team of well-trained professionals to successfully teach children so that they learn to the second power in an enriched learning environment. Educating children is a team sport. Become a team player and communicate with the other players. This will help you establish and maintain credibility with these groups of individuals. You are making every effort to involve and update people who are part of the learning team for each child.

A major flaw of many teachers is that we do not network. I am always amazed to visit with individuals from other professions who do this as part of their daily routine. While I am fumbling in my purse for a business card, they are already standing with theirs in hand. They have names, numbers, and addresses readily available in a Palm Pilot or other organizer when I am trying to find a specific Post-it note with information scribbled on it in my office. Teachers need to emulate networking skills from other professions and use them.

COMMUNICATING WITH PARENTS

As a classroom teacher, community volunteer, or religious teacher, communicate on a regular basis with the children's parents. I suggest a weekly newsletter that goes home the same day each week. When you show consistency, parents will get into the routine of always checking the backpack on that day. (I also recommend sending home graded work on that same day.) Create a newsletter using your favorite computer program. Always give parents information about future events so they can mark them on a calendar at home. I once worked with a first-year teacher who worked hard each week to tell parents about what they had done that week. I explained that the parents needed advance notice. Include somewhere on your page the school website address, your school e-mail address, and the school fax number. This information can become part of your template.

Need some supplies for a cooking project, a center, or items to celebrate the 100th day of school? Include this information in your weekly newsletter. Invite parents to attend an assembly. Give them advance notice about an upcoming test or project that will be due. Provide them with information not only for the next week, but also for major events that are coming in the future.

One suggestion regarding the newsletter or calendar: Create a folder on your computer and save each week's calendar or newsletter. If you are required to submit an end-of-the-year report, you could include this information in that report. You can copy samples and include them in your professional portfolio. If or when you apply for a job at another location, you can show samples as evidence of your efforts to communicate with parents. This will be very impressive to interviewers.

Security suggestion regarding the newsletter or calendar: Because of confidentiality issues, FERPA, and basic security issues, refrain from putting the child's first and last name in the communication.

Many teachers want to add the names of children who are celebrating birthdays. They also want to announce the arrival of a new student who has joined the classroom. Either use the first name only or initials, or omit the topic. (The same is true when identifying student lockers or cubbyholes. An identification number or combination of letters and numbers will provide security for every child. If the lockers are in the hallway, anyone can read the child's name.)

In today's society, many children stay in more than one household throughout the week. Why not send home *two* newsletters with children who are part of a joint custody arrangement? (And when progress reports go home, send home two sets. And when grade cards go home, send home two sets. Go the extra mile to accommodate both parents. Create a win-win-win situation!) That way each parent or household will be abreast of the events and happenings at school as well as in your class. It helps to maintain a great working relationship between households and school.

Do you have a game plan for welcoming new students throughout the year? Save all those extra handouts teachers get from the office during the first week. Organize the papers by sets and put each set into a large yellow envelope. This will include written information such as lunch prices, school calendar, and so on. Make a telephone call to the new parents at the end of the week. Answer any questions that the parents might have. Tell them that you have sent home special information that will be helpful to them. Tell them that you will be sending home a weekly communication on a specific day—which will include the school's website information, your e-mail address, and the school fax number. They will appreciate your communication efforts. They will be reading the information from the yellow envelope that evening. They will be looking for the weekly communication. They have been brought up to speed quickly and professionally. What a marvelous first impression you have made with these new parents!

If your school has a policy for parents sending e-mails to school, send it home to the parents at the beginning of the year. If there is no policy, please consider one for yourself. You might specify that if the parents have a pressing concern, they should call the school and leave a telephone message. It may be something that can be solved by the administrative assistants in the office. Because you will be teaching and working with children for the majority of your time at school, you will not be constantly checking e-mail. Another item to stress is no forwarding. Although forwarded e-mails may be cute or funny, you don't have time for them in the work place. Design your own "netiquette policy" if your district does not have one—and make it known to your parents.

COMMUNICATING WITH COLLEAGUES

Communicate with your colleagues. You may have just read a super article that a teacher down the hall would love to read. You may have just learned about a marvelous seminar or workshop that is coming to your area. Share this information with colleagues—and they will start to share with you. I often send this information in the form of an e-mail to my colleagues because we are at three different campuses.

COMMUNICATING WITH OTHER PROFESSIONALS

Communicate with other professionals at your school site such as the school nurse, the librarian, the counselor, the special services teachers who share responsibilities for teaching your students, and other specialty teachers such as the computer teacher or the music teacher. To best serve your students, you need to be in contact and communication with other professionals at your site. It takes a team effort to successfully educate a child. Become a team player.

COMMUNICATING WITH ADMINISTRATORS

Communicate with your administrators. Let them know the topics or units you are working on with the children. Visit with them about various professional development areas you would like to pursue.

Inquire about possible financial assistance or supplies for future projects for your class. This can be done the old-fashioned way by talking with your administrator. Verbal conversations can sometimes be forgotten. Due to time constraints on both parties, you might wish to send a short e-mail update or request. That way you know that things were put in writing, and the message can be saved or reviewed at a later date. Messages to or from your administrator can also be forwarded on to other individuals who may be able to provide additional information or assistance to you.

- Summary for administrators: If your district does not have a "netiquette" or e-mail policy, work with the faculty to create one for your school site. This will alleviate wasted messages such as forwarded e-mail. Because the policy is in writing and given to each household, parents will be less likely to make infractions.

  Encourage *every* teacher to send home a communication in the form of a newsletter or calendar *every* week. While you are encouraging communication, why not select a specific target day that the information is sent home? The parents will be impressed with the coordination efforts of the school and appreciate the consistency. What a wonderful reputation!

  Do your part in the effort to communicate—with parents, colleagues, and faculty and staff. Remember that verbal communications are frequently forgotten. E-mail versions can be sent quickly and efficiently without using paper. They can be saved and reviewed if necessary. And you have documentation of your communication efforts. You may need samples for your portfolio or to show to a future interviewer as well.

  Make efforts to create a school newsletter or calendar with schoolwide events. Send this home on a regular basis.

  Make efforts to keep the school web page current. Work with your webmaster to update the web page on a regular basis. Provide him or her with information about future events. Give your teachers and staff target dates by which they may submit information for the web page. Put the web page address on all communications that go home. Encourage your teachers to follow the same practice.

Teaching is a team effort, and you are the leader of that team.

- Summary for teachers: Make every effort to communicate with parents, colleagues, other professionals at your site, and your administrators. Send home multiple sets of communications when applicable.

Keep copies of your communications in a folder on your computer. This can be used for future reports or future needs.

Network, network, network! Take cues from professionals in other occupations. Keep in contact with other teachers throughout your district as well as across the nation. You will be connected with the newest cutting-edge practices in the profession. You will be aware of summer seminars, various grant opportunities, and ways in which you can beef up your professional development. You and your students will benefit from your networking endeavors.

- Summary for homeschool parents: Consider making a calendar or master schedule with your child each week as part of the learning opportunity. Make this a teachable moment each week. Post this calendar or schedule in a prominent place in your home.

Network with other homeschool parents in your area. You may find a university or other group to help provide learning opportunities and answer your questions. There may also be online sources for you. Network, network, network.

- Summary for community and religious volunteers: The same suggestions for classroom teachers are true for you as well. You need to make every effort to communicate with your children's parents. Keep them posted about future events or items that you need donated for special projects.

Continue to network with colleagues. You can share ideas. You will learn about seminars or workshops that would be of benefit to you and your students.

If you have a direct supervisor, keep in contact with him or her as well. This person will be a wonderful resource for you.

CONNECTING
THE DOTS:
LEARNING STYLES

13

BEFORE CONNECTING THE DOTS: SETTING OBJECTIVES— DESIGNING A PLAN

The art of teaching is the art of assisting discovery.

—Mark Van Doren

Before starting to connect the dots and create marvelous learning opportunities for your students, you need to set the learning outcomes or learning objectives. You may also hear these referred to as teaching objectives. Whatever the term, you need to establish measurable objectives to create an assessment to evaluate if learning has indeed occurred and to what degree the content has been learned—you want to create an evaluation to get a number grade or percentage in the grade book.

The objective is the cornerstone of your teaching lessons. All aspects of your lesson revolve around the objective. Once the objective is established, everything else will begin to flow.

As educators—whether you are a homeschool teacher, a religious teacher, a community volunteer, or a classroom teacher—use *measurable* objectives when writing your learning outcome. Verbs that are subjective or ambiguous will make the assessment process difficult if not impossible.

Use concrete verbs rather than abstract ones. Students can always describe a fork, plate, or drinking glass. They are stumped when trying to explain liberty, freedom, or justice. A fork is concrete to children.

Freedom, although we dearly love, value, and appreciate it, is difficult for even adults to describe. It's really tough for children. Freedom is abstract. When you select concrete verbs for your teaching and learning objectives, you will know and your supervisors will know exactly your intentions.

Here are my top-of-the-chart all-time *worst* verbs for learning objectives to use when writing your learning or teaching objectives. Avoid these verbs like the plague.

All-Time Worst Verbs for Learning Objectives

- Appreciate
- Become acquainted with
- Believe
- Be aware of
- Comprehend
- Develop an understanding of
- Enjoy
- Have a knowledge of
- Increase interest in
- Know
- Perceive
- Realize
- Recognize
- Share
- Think
- Understand
- Value

Bloom's Taxonomy (Bloom, 1984) is widely used in writing teaching and learning objectives. A taxonomy is a system of hierarchical classification. In 1956 (that's right, it has been around for 5 decades!), Benjamin Bloom headed a group of educational psychologists. Together, they developed a classification of levels of thinking behaviors thought to be important in the processes of learning.

Most writers explain Bloom's Taxonomy by starting with the lowest level of thinking and moving to the highest levels. I will work backwards. As a visual learner, this is most concrete for me. The first three categories are designed for higher level thinking. The final three categories are designed for lower level thinking. Keep this in mind as we review the basic elements of Bloom's Taxonomy.

- *Evaluation* is to establish criteria and make judgments and decisions.
- *Synthesis* is to create a new whole, see a new pattern of relationships, develop a new and unusual approach.
- *Analysis* is the ability to break facts, ideas, and concepts into parts, to examine relationships among parts, to compare and contrast, and to create categories.
- *Application* is the ability to apply understanding to new situations and solve problems.
- *Comprehension* is the ability to explain, interpret, and extrapolate ideas, concepts, and information.
- *Knowledge* refers to the memory of facts and information.

Table 13.1 shows Bloom's Taxonomy from the highest level to the lowest level. Included in this table are the suggested verbs for each criterion.

As previously mentioned, Bloom's Taxonomy has been the gold standard for educators writing objectives for the past 5 decades. I always tell my teacher education candidates to use a verb from Bloom to write their objectives. I stress how the verb must be measurable, objective, concrete, and so on. Then a bright and brilliant student will ask, "How can we measure a verb like *discuss?*" Or a genius-level future teacher will say, "I don't understand how to evaluate 'explain' or 'generalize' or 'judge.'" I agree! So I have had to go through Bloom's Taxonomy and delete a few verbs that do not fit the "measurable, objective, concrete" mold. The following list of verbs from Bloom's Taxonomy do fit that mold. Please *use* verbs from this list when designing your objective.

CHAPTER 13

Table 13.1.   Bloom's Taxonomy

		Evaluation			
Appraise	Conclude	Contrast	Critique	Grade	Judge
Justify	Interpret	Support	Recommend		

		Synthesis			
Arrange	Combine	Compile	Construct	Create	Design
Formulate	Generalize	Generate	Group	Integrate	Organize
Relate	Summarize				

		Analysis	
Diagram	Differentiate	Discriminate	Outline
Relate	Separate	Subdivide	

		Application	
Change	Compute	Construct	Demonstrate
Illustrate	Predict	Relate	Solve

		Comprehension			
Classify	Compare	Convert	Contrast	Discuss	Distinguish
Estimate	Explain	Generalize	Give examples		Infer
Interpret	Paraphrase	Rewrite	Summarize	Translate	

		Knowledge				
Count	Define	Identify	Label	List	Match	Name
Outline	Point Out	Quote	Recite	Repeat	Reproduce	Select
State	Trace					

Source: Adapted from Kellough, 1996

Measurable Verbs from Bloom's Taxonomy

Arrange	Define	Match	Select
Classify	Design	Name	Separate
Combine	Diagram	Outline	State
Compare	Estimate	Predict	Subdivide
Compute	Group	Quote	Summarize
Contrast	Identify	Reproduce	Solve
Construct	Infer	Replicate	Trace
Convert	Label	Rewrite	Translate
Count	List		
Create			

Other taxonomies have been developed for other types of learning. Krathwohl, Bloom, and Masia (1964) developed a taxonomy for the affective domain, which focused on feelings, beliefs, or values. These areas are not the primary focus for classroom teachers targeting learning. Another taxonomy was developed by Harrow (1977) that targeted the psychomotor domain. This domain was originally of interest to physical education teachers or early childhood teachers. Often it was used when they were dealing with fine or gross motor skills. Today, with the use of performance tasks or projects as part of our daily teaching, this domain is used by creative and innovative teachers at all teaching levels. The four primary areas of Harrow's Taxonomy are movement, manipulation, communicating, and creating.

The information below shows the Psychomotor Taxonomy along with teaching/learning objectives.

Psychomotor Taxonomy
Adapted from Harrow (1977)

Movement   Gross motor coordination
Verbs—adjust, carry, clean, locate, manipulate, obtain, walk
Sample objective: The student will be able to **manipulate** a hand-held calculator.

Manipulation   Fine motor coordination
Verbs—assemble, build, calibrate, connect, focus, thread
Sample objective: The student will be able to **focus** the microscope correctly.

Communicating   Communication of ideas and feelings
Verbs—analyze, ask, describe, draw, explain, write
Sample objective: The student will be able to **draw** an obtuse angle.

Creating   Represents student's coordination of thinking, learning, and behaving
Verbs—create, design, invent
Sample objective: The student will be able to use discarded materials from the environment to **design** an environment for an imaginary animal that he or she has mentally created.

FORMULA FOR WRITING AN OBJECTIVE

Teachers are required to write out their objectives. It is part of their evaluation from the administration. I recommend that homeschool teachers, religious teachers, and community volunteers follow this practice. There is a special formula for writing an objective. Begin with "the students will be able to:" each time you write an objective. You then fill in the verb that you want them to achieve when they have completed the learning opportunity or lesson. Then follow this with your description. For the evaluation to connect with the objective, you must sometimes add a number. The following objective illustrates this.

> The students will be able to: List three animals that are part of the *ursa* genus.
> Answers could include the polar bear, the black bear, the grizzly bear, or the brown bear. But they only need to list three because you have specified that in your objective. When you grade the answers, you look for three that are correct. This extra attention to detail always pays off. Compare the above objective with the following:
> The students will be able to: List animals that are part of the *ursa* genus.
> How will you grade the students' work? What criteria will you use? The verb *list* describes a super simple task for children; however, it becomes less objective and more subjective—less concrete and more abstract—when you fail to go the extra mile and specify the exact number you require.

The formula for writing a successful teaching/learning objective includes the statement "The students will be able to:" plus a concrete verb for something measurable plus a precise description of the students' requirements.

I always encourage teachers to create their own plan books. Everyone has a special schedule with pullouts and various lunch times and duty assignments. Creating a template that can be filled in each day saves the busy teacher tons of time. Before proceeding, visit with your administrator about this project. Show her or him samples that you have designed. Photocopy them, three-hole-punch the pages, and clamp them into a three-ring binder. You may want to take the pages to a photocopy store and have things professionally bound—with a plastic cover on the front and back. In the spaces for the objectives, in advance type in "The students will be able to:" You will be off to a great start on the objective. Use the formula to complete things successfully.

It has been stated previously that all aspects of the lesson revolve around the objective. The final chapter of this book examines the evaluation or assessment process. You may wish to skip to that chapter to continue reading on this topic. Just as the assessment connects with the objective, so do the introduction, the instruction, and the conclusion. All aspects pivot around your stated objective; therefore, use careful consideration when selecting your verb and completing the objective. Attention to details of the objective will help to promote long-term learning for your students, and that is the goal of all teachers.

The objective is of paramount importance. You also need to complete your teaching plan. The degree of detail depends on your teaching position. The classroom teacher has been trained to create plans. It is part of the job requirement, and the administrator will check periodically to be certain that this is being done. The religious teacher or community volunteer does not create a full-blown plan; however, creating a modified plan will be valuable. When you fail to plan, you plan to fail.

The components for a lesson plan for the classroom teacher depend on the requirements of your administrators or district. The religious teacher or community volunteer would benefit from following the Before, During, and After model. After determining the objective, decide what *you* will do before the lesson, during the lesson, and after the lesson. Jot down your required actions. Use your notes during your lesson. You might have distractions and interruptions. Having the information in writing will be helpful to you. It will assist you in providing the best possible learning opportunity for the students.

Rather than a full-blown plan, I create an agenda for each class session. Why would a university professor need information for a class in writing? Because when you fail to plan, you plan to fail! Our classes meet once per week and last 2 hours and 40 minutes. I detail the supplies I need to bring, and I write out exactly what information will be placed on the whiteboard for the students' information. (I color-code the whiteboard. One color represents today's events, another color represents what we will be doing next week, still another color is for up-and-coming events at the university.) I create a step-by-step approach that I will take during the class meeting, and I write out my summation and any additional information students will need for the next class meeting. The students have a calendar of events that they receive the first week of the semester that lists in writing the information that they need for each week. Rather than creating a calendar of events for the entire semester, why not create one for a month? You can discuss the information with the children and send it home to the parents.

- Summary for administrators: Supply your faculty with a list of super verbs to use when writing teaching/learning objectives at the beginning of the school year. Give them samples of the way you require the lesson plans to be written. Tell them or put in writing your policy about checking the plan books—how often, specific day of the week, once a quarter—whatever it is, let the faculty know.

  When you conduct your "new teacher" seminar at the beginning of the year, specify your criteria before they ever write their first objective. Then check their plan books frequently over the first month of school to be sure they are complying.

  Encourage your faculty to design their own plan books that meet the needs of their schedules. They can photocopy the templates and put them in a three-ring binder or have them bound at a photocopy store.
- Summary for teachers: Follow the formula in this chapter to successfully write an objective. Use the verbs recommended in this chapter.

Visit with your administrator about creating your own plan book. I suggest that you use plastic covers for the front and back if you have things professionally bound. This will allow you to wipe off any sneezes or spills and keep things clean and hygienic.

- Summary for homeschool parents: Where will you keep your objectives? You can design a template for your objectives just as the classroom teacher does.

  Follow the formula and use the verbs in the book for successful objectives.

  Use the Before, During, and After model to create an agenda for your lesson. It will be beneficial to you and your children.

- Summary for community and religious volunteers: You will not be responsible for writing all the elements of a lesson plan, but writing a successful objective will keep you on track when you work with your students. This will also be a framework when you reflect on your lesson.

  Using the Before, During, and After model to write down an agenda or modified plan will be helpful to you.

REFERENCES

Bloom, B. S. (Ed.) (1984). *Taxonomy of educational objectives, Book 1: Cognitive domain.* White Plains, NY: Longman.

Harrow. A. J. (1977). *Taxonomy of psychomotor domain.* White Plains, NY: Longman.

Krathwohl, D. R., Bloom, B. S., & Masia, B. B. (1964). *Taxonomy of educational goals: Handbook II. Affective domain.* New York: McKay.

14

LANGUAGE ARTS

I touch the future. I teach.

—Christa McAuliffe

Chapters 14, 15, and 16 include suggestions for applying the infor-mation in the previous chapters. Although I tried to group this information, some of the suggestions flow over into other curricular areas; therefore, read chapters 14, 15, and 16 carefully. You will find super ideas that you can change slightly to meet the needs of your students and result in long-term learning or learning[2]. You may also decide to take an idea and use it with still another curricular area.

In chapters 14, 15, and 16 teachers and homeschool parents will learn cost-effective teaching strategies that promote learning using the three learning styles. Administrators will appreciate the inexpen-sive ways to promote student learning and also the attention to stu-dent safety. Religious teachers and community volunteers will find a gold mine of suggestions that they can transpose to the learning needs of their students. Homeschool parents will find not only wonderful learning opportunities for your children in a homeschool enriched learning environment, but also some great ideas to take on travel ex-cursions by car or plane or things to do over the summer vacation.

Color can be added to these activities so that the students acquire the information faster and retain it longer. I am still in the "black permanent marker" phase of life. Today, however, the students have access to gel pens as well as permanent markers in a myriad of colors (yes, they still make black!). As you read the contents of chapters 14, 15, and 16, think outside the box regarding color. Your students will benefit from your insight.

As you read these chapters, consider how you can utilize the contents from the previous chapters. How can you include music with this idea? How would you interject movement with this project? You are the creative and innovative leader of the class. You add what is needed to provide an enriched learning environment for your students.

LANGUAGE ARTS—WRITING—SPELLING

Why Start the Lesson on Monday?

It is early Monday morning, time for every elementary student to write their spelling words X number of times. The spelling test will be Friday. Why? Why can't the new words be introduced Wednesday or Thursday? This would give students extra days over the weekend to study. (Some of us are not natural spellers and need the extra days.) The goal of spelling is to learn how to spell those words. The students should be able to spell them the folloing week, the following month, not just for a test the same week they were introduced. Extra time and exposure to words will promote true learning of them. It will also help alleviate test anxiety. The students will be more confident—because they have truly learned the words.

Chain/Spelling Chain

The next "Why?" is why do they have to write those words over and over? If we can put people on the moon, can't we build a better mousetrap regarding spelling? One alternative is to use rainbow spelling, discussed in chapter 8. This activity uses color to enhance learning. It also utilizes the kinesthetic and visual learning styles. A second alternative is to create a "spelling chain."

Materials: photocopy paper cut into strips or links using a paper cutter, colored pencil or colored markers, and tape or a stapler to connect the links.

Students write the spelling word on one link of the chain. They continue to create links and then tape them or staple them together to create a chain. The chain can remain long or can be connected to make a circle—or necklace or bracelet if they wish. Again, color can be used with this activity.

This activity is a great example of transferability—it can be transferred to *any* curricular area. Besides spelling words, students can write vocabulary words and terms or math facts on the links. You can do this activity with all ages. I have used this idea with elementary students as well as adult learners at the university. I am always amused seeing the students wearing chain bracelets after the activity is finished. This is not something that is tossed in the trash or out the bus window on the way home. They keep this and they like to display it. This is a simple, yet effective, learning activity. Community volunteers or religious leaders can easily adapt the chain activity for their learning activities. Homeschool parents can utilize this throughout the week to enhance learning in various curricular areas.

ABC or Alphabet Box

These can be designed for virtually *any* topic in *any* curricular area. Although this idea appears in the language arts chapter, please use this for science and social studies with your students. You can design the template by creating a page with 26 boxes. One alphabet letter is to be placed in each box. The students will then write words that begin with each letter and relate to the topic of the boxes. As the teacher, let the students know if they can write more than one word per letter. Many students may wish to draw a picture to go along with the word. By using paper larger than the standard size of photocopy paper, they will have enough room to add their illustrations. Some letters are very difficult to connect with a specific word about a topic—such as X. As the classroom teacher, you might want to allow them to leave a certain number of letters blank. Tell them prior to beginning the project. This can be an ongoing process while they study a specific topic, or it could be an assessment at the end of a unit.

As with any curricular suggestion, consider having the teacher be the "recorder" the first time students are exposed to ABC or alphabet boxes. Once they understand the concept, older students can work independently or in small groups.

ABC or alphabet boxes can be a substitute for a word wall for the entire classroom or a word page for individual students.

Table 14.1 is an example of an ABC or alphabet box on the topic of football.

Materials: photocopy paper used as a template—legal or ledger size works great as does the standard size—pencil, colored pencils, markers.

Elements of a Children's Narrative Story

There are several different types of children's books. The standard narrative story consists of four components:

1. Plot
2. Characters
3. Setting
4. Conflict/resolution or problem/solution

Recall your favorite children's fairy tales. They all have the components mentioned above. Who are the characters in "Cinderella" or "The Three Little Pigs"? Perhaps the setting is as general as "once upon a time," but at least we can conclude that the story took place in the past tense. In children's narrative stories there is always a problem or conflict between or among the characters or with the setting. An example of a conflict with the setting would be seen in a book about the Dust Bowl or a snow storm. The problem or conflict always has a solution or resolution—it is resolved at the end. And how do fairy tales end? They all lived happily ever after. Children's narrative story plots do not all end on a happy note, but the problem or conflict is solved—very often by the main child character.

Table 14.1. Example of an ABC or Alphabet Box on the Topic of Football

A	B	C	D	E	F
American League	ball	coach	defense	end zone	football
athlete	block	catch		end	field
astroturf	Big 12 conference	cheerleader		ESPN	field goal
all-American		conversion			fake
		chain crew			fake punt
					fans

G	H	I	J	K	L
goal	helmet	interception	jump	kick	lateral
guard	hike	I-back		kick off	linebacker
goal line	Heisman	injury			lineman
grass field	huddle	I-formation			
	half time				

M	N	O	P	Q	R
money	nose guard	offense	punt	quarterback	referee
men	NFL	Orange Bowl	player	quick kick	return
middle-linebacker		out-of-bounds	pass	quarters	receiver
mascot		overtime	pigskin		running back
motion			place kick		roster
Monday night football					roommate
					rule book

S	T	U	V	W	X
safety	touchdown	umpire	victory	wide receiver	X-back
sidelines	tickets	up backs		win	X-man
stadium	tackle			wing back	
sky box	tee			wind direction	
Southeast Conference	time out			water boy	
	two-point conversion				

Y	Z
yards	Z-back
yardage	
Y-back	

Source: Adapted from Farris (2004).

Once students recognize these elements, they can begin writing their own narrative story. We worked on a fun activity in class one week, and after the students shared their project, they then showed us the children's narrative book that they used. As humans, we assumed that the characters were people, with names like Susan or Chrysanthemum. We were soon surprised when the characters were a family of mice or rabbits. Often authors will select an animal as a character and give him or her human qualities such as speaking, singing, or walking on two legs. The Tawny Scrawny Lion and Arthur are two examples.

The elements of the story can be arranged in a graphic organizer such as a concept map (discussed later in this chapter). They can also be used to create student books such as a flip book or shape book. You could transfer the elements of a narrative story onto links of a chain, as discussed previously in the chapter. Different colors could be used to categorize each group within the story . . . and they lived happily ever after!

Chunking

A great way to introduce the spelling words is by "chunking." You examine each word and try to find a "word within a word." If a spelling word was *today*, you would examine the word and discover that *to* and *day* are both found within that word—two chunks make up that word. Most students already have those two words within their spelling repertoire. This new word becomes two familiar words that make the spelling word easy to master within the designated time frame. Chunking is a great way to help visual learners see the words within words. When writing the words the student can also write the chunked word a different color from the other letters of the word. For example, re**port**er. (I used bold type to depict the chunked portion.)

Chunking is done each day with numbers. When you give your birthday in six numbers, you are chunking your month, day of birth, and year of birth (last two digits). Adults know what those six digits mean. It is difficult to remember seven numbers, but when you remember your telephone number you break them down into the first three followed by the last four. No one can recall nine numbers, but through chunking, our social security numbers are broken down into three, two, and four numbers. We can write them or say them easily by chunking them.

Turn the Paper Sideways

Another way to help students learn spelling words is by asking them to write the words one time by turning their paper sideways. This provides a single space (line) for each letter. The first time students try this activity, they will need some help getting their heading on their paper. It still goes in the same spot—there's just not a margin at the top of the page. This is a simple variation that appeals to the visual learner. It's a fun diversion from the traditional Monday morning writing of the words. Rainbow spelling can be easily incorporated into this activity.

Turning the paper sideways is also a super way to help students with specific mathematical functions. It is a good organizational aid for elementary students computing column addition problems. It also works well for doing problems with place value and especially decimal problems. Students can align the problems using the lines on the paper. Just as rainbow spelling can be used for language arts activities that use notebook paper turned sideways, it can also be used with math problems.

Spelling and Water

A fun kinesthetic activity for students involves using wax paper and a toothpick. Advanced preparation requires the teacher to tear off wax paper sheets in advance. A small amount of water is also required for each group of students. A common straw can be used as an eyedropper. Put the straw into the water, cover the top of the straw, and then squeeze the straw to put one drop on the wax paper. The students "write" their words using the toothpick. This works for both printing and cursive writing. A variation of this is to write the words on plain photocopy paper. Put that paper underneath the wax paper. The student can see the letters. They trace each letter by dragging the water drop around the wax paper. To add an extra touch, the student could use colored markers to write the words on the photocopy paper. Another twist is to use a drop of food coloring in the water. As we have already learned, when you use color the students grasp the information faster and retain it longer. As with all classroom activities, safety is paramount. The teacher should pass out and collect the toothpicks. Cleanup from this activity is quick and easy. This activity is also cost-effective.

Shapes

One year I was teaching a self-contained sixth grade. I went to a conference in the middle of the year that demonstrated this activity. I have used it with various grade levels ever since. It's adaptable to all curricular areas and all topics. The teacher needs a simple outline shape. I used shapes to connect to the seasons or topics related to each month. For example, in March we could use the outline shape of a kite, a shamrock, a rainbow, and lion or lamb (March comes in like a lion and goes out like a lamb). I would check clip art from the Internet and also look through children's coloring books for the shapes.

Materials: paperclip (or restickable glue stick as opposed to a permanent glue stick), clean page of photocopy paper, sheet with outline printed on it.

You place the clean page on top of the printed page and attach it with a paperclip or using the glue. Next, the students can write their spelling words around the shape, which is visible through the paper. Cursive writing works best, but words can also be printed.

A variation of this activity is to use notebook paper on top of the printed page. The students can write *around* the shape and also write *on* the lines. This allows more room for writing. A final variation is to write only on the lines and then trace around the outline shape. Colored pens or markers can be used during the writing process.

Aside from writing spelling words, the students can write vocabulary words and definitions for science, social studies, or math. The shape can become a shape book, and the lined paper can be used for the student to write journal entries. I hope that this will become an old standard for you and your students.

Macaroni and Cereal

A fun kinesthetic and visual activity for students is to use alphabet cereal or alphabet macaroni. Please have a contrasting background available for the students to best see the manipulatives.

Materials: dark background such as a dark piece of construction paper, alphabet macaroni or alphabet cereal, resealable bag to store the manipulatives. Optional: coffee filters to hold the manipulatives during the activity.

Give the students a set of manipulatives and ask them to select the letters to spell the spelling words or vocabulary words. You can call out a word orally for a large group activity. This can be put on audiotape and used as a language arts center activity.

A spin-off activity is to give the students a large set of manipulatives and ask them to spell words within a specific time frame. This could be an independent or small-group activity.

I have used this activity with upper elementary students. Prior to the activity explain that the manipulatives are not food. They are to be used as manipulatives. Please ask the students not to bite off the leg of an R to make a P. The manipulatives are not to be eaten.

Collect all the manipulatives and store them in resealable bags. I suggest that you place these in a large hard plastic container that is mouse-proof and insect-proof. I speak from experience on the necessity for this measure.

Cereal can also be used in mathematics. The various pieces of cereal can be used to line up side by side to create geometric shapes. You can also use various types of cereal in grouping or sorting or ordering activities with preschool and primary students. Many teachers will use various buttons for these activities. Cereal is a readily available, reusable, low-cost manipulative that takes the place of the buttons.

Graphs can be created using various types of cereal. This works well when the cereal is placed on notebook paper turned sideways.

CHAPTER 14

Students can use the lines to keep categories divided and also aligned. I used M&M's with my university students to create data distribution tables in a junior-level statistics class. (Yes, at the university level I asked the students to shift their notebook paper so it was running sideways and the lines were vertical. Students can benefit from this practice whatever their age.) Cereal could have been substituted for this activity.

Story Cards

You can create story cards using clip art, scrapbook stickers, regular stickers, magazine and newspaper photos, fabric, and any other form of visual you wish to use. I have used card stock and also craft foam as the backing for these cards and cut the background into fourths. The card stock can be laminated and kept clean easily. You can use visuals that revolve around a theme, such as back to school, or something completely unrelated. The choice is yours. There is no established number for a set of story cards. You may wish to use a number that is high enough so that every student in your class has one card. You can certainly have smaller numbers within sets if you choose to use this as a center activity.

Materials: set of story cards, one classroom or group of students.

The story will be a group project. The students are required to listen, and when their turn is called, they will use the contents of their card to tell a portion of the story. The teacher begins the story with a great beginning, for example, "It was a dark and stormy night at the zoo." Or another great starter is "It was a bright and sunny day at the beach." The teacher then points to a student who continues part of the story. The teacher may wish to add a transitional phrase such as "and then" or "but suddenly" or "in the twinkling of an eye" and then point to another student. At the end of the story before the last student shares, the teacher might say, "but we knew everything would be alright because . . ." The final student will conclude the story.

The key to this story is listening. Yes, it promotes creative thinking, but if the student repeats a portion of the story that has already been shared everyone will catch that he or she was not listening. Also there will be a huge delay if the student has not listened and does not know what to add to the story. Listening by all students is critical to the success of the story.

A great aspect of this project is that every story will be different. You can use the same cards with the same group of students, but because each student has a different card, the contents of the story will still be different.

You can use story cards to have students tell the story orally, and then you can ask them to write the story that the class just created. They are now listening and then writing. Or you could stop the story in the middle and ask the students to finish the story. You have many options.

I have used this activity with students while we were getting ready for lunch. The usual loiterers and dawdlers in the restroom quickly returned so they wouldn't miss too much of the story. We would also use this activity at the end of the day if we had extra time. Teachers have told me that they created several sets and used them the day before winter holiday vacation. Others have told me that they used them the day before spring break. It's a great filler but also a good language arts activity any day of the school year. I liked to use different colored card stock or different patterned or colored craft foam for each set. That helped me to keep the sets in order. I also kept each set in a resealable bag for easy storage and organization. Community volunteers and religious leaders could use this activity at the beginning of their time to give the students a time to listen intently and participate.

WWWWH Cards—Who? When? What? Where? How? Cards or Interrogative Cards

To create these cards, cut card stock or craft foam into fourths, or you may wish to create large cards using an entire sheet of stock or foam per card. Using a permanent marker, write the words Who? When? What? Where? How? or How much? or How many? on the cards. Write the words large so the students can see them when you hold them up. As you are discussing a story from the reader or discussing a historical event in social studies, hold up the cards and ask the students to answer the questions. A fun deviation is to pass out the cards to random students in the classroom. Ask them to show their card as the discussion develops. They can then answer the question or ask another student to provide the answer. Imagine a mathematics lesson where the story problems are answered using How much? How many? or How? (how did you get your answer?). WWWWH Cards can be used with all curricular areas.

Word Walls

Word walls are a great addition to the learning environment, whether they are for a homeschool setting, a classroom setting, or the room where the students gather for community groups or religious training. The purpose of the word wall is to provide proper spelling that the students can refer to when they are writing. Word walls also can be used to help the teacher review various vocabulary words or terms with the students. Because the words are highly and continuously visible to the students, they are saturated with visual stimulation in an enriched environment.

Materials: strips of cash register tape or slips of paper, magic markers (black and also various colors).

You have various options when setting up a word wall. You can categorize your words by themes or by the seasons. Many word walls consist of words that all reflect the same theme, such as back to school or autumn. A difficult but effective way is by alphabetical order. You may wish to categorize them by topics and by color. Each grouping would be written in a different color. You might want to include the vocabulary words from the science, mathematics, and social studies chapters on your word wall. These would be easy to distinguish when you use different colors. Cash register tape is easy to use because you can vary the lengths but the strips will remain the same width. You may wish to use your technology skills and type your words using a word processor. This would be an easy way to print out the words uniformly and also an easy way to use color.

Carpet Samples and Tiles

This is a great visual and kinesthetic activity that can be used for several curricular areas. You may use foam or purchased plastic tiles or 1-inch bathroom and kitchen tiles.

Materials: foam or plastic tiles or 1-inch commercial tiles (ceramic tiles), looped portions of Velcro, carpet samples that are looped, permanent marker if you use commercial tiles. Note: Shag or cut carpet will not work for this project; also, many carpet and tile stores have extra pieces of the 1-inch tiles that they will give away.

If you are using commercial tiles, cut them apart first. Then use a marker to write either single-digit numbers or lower- or uppercase letters. If this is going to be a math project, you may wish to create "function" tiles such as −, +, = and so on. Cut short pieces of Velcro and attach them to the back side of the tile. Caution: If you are using commercial tiles, they will be razor sharp if they are chipped or broken. Please dispose of any tiles in this condition. They will also break if they are dropped on a hard floor.

This project can be a small-group activity or a center activity. The carpet samples can be placed on top of the students' desks. They will be at a good level for spelling, writing sentences, and computing mathematical questions.

Magnetic Paint/Magnets

An activity similar to the carpet samples and tiles involves magnetic paint and magnets.

Materials: magnetic paint (there are numerous products on the market today), your choice of (a) inexpensive letters and numbers with magnets attached or (b) letters and numbers (remember to have math functions available so they know to add, divide, etc.) or (c) tiles with magnet tape attached to the back side—you will need to purchase a role of magnetic tape and use old scissors.

Before undertaking this project, visit with your building-level principal. You need to have administrative approval before proceeding.

Examine your classroom carefully. Decide on the best spot for independent or small-group student learning that will be least distracting to other students. Consider the optimal working height for your students. You need to examine both the longitude and latitude of your classroom. If they cannot reach this space, bring it down to their level. Then follow the manufacturer's directions to paint this area. This is a great project for reviewing the arrangement of your classroom. You may wish to move furniture and completely rearrange your learning environment to best serve the students.

One of my former students decided to paint the wall space directly below the chalkboard/whiteboard area. This space is rarely used. It also has to be an area with free access to the board; therefore, you would not put any furniture or storage furniture in this area. The students were able to sit or lie down on the floor and use this area for independent or small-group work. They had numbers, letters, and other task tiles such as prefixes, suffixes, and blends to use in this area. Note: I am always preaching about incorporating the use of color in learning activities. I am always concerned about providing contrast between the background and the manipulatives. This learning area was painted hot pink. What a fun idea for second graders!

If you are making your manipulatives, you can use foam letters and numbers cut out of craft foam and attach magnetic tape to the back side. I pull the tape off the back for a few inches and then cut the tape into 3/8-inch pieces. This is much easier than attempting to remove the backing from such a tiny piece.

Another great suggestion for your manipulatives is to examine children's placemats. These are usually less than $1.00 to purchase and have some colorful learning activities on either or both sides. I have seen such topics as the solar system, money, days of the week/months, letters and numbers, and maps. I made a learning center using two placemats that had information about the presidents. Because good information was printed on both sides, I had to purchase two identical placemats. One side had the pictures with their names and the other side had facts about each president. I keep each group of information in a resealable bag, and everything goes inside a clean metal paint can. The can becomes the canvas for the learning center. The students can use the lid or the bottom or the curved sides of the can to attach their manipulative pieces. Thought: You can use one large can to hold various sets of manipulatives.

I have seen teachers use magnetic manipulatives along with an old cookie sheet or metal tray at learning centers. These can be picked up at garage sales for a low cost. Another suggestion that a student gave me was to use metal flashing. This would have to be taped or bound around the edges to ensure student safety. The flashing could be mounted onto the wall, with administrative approval. It could also be cut into smaller pieces, such as the size of a cookie sheet or tray, with protection around the edges. Student safety is paramount.

Cereal Stories

One rainy summer day my niece called with a desperate request. Her three children were all home and they had invited others over to play. Because it was raining, all the children were in the house! I told her to get out the following materials:

Materials: cereal boxes from the pantry, glue, some markers, and cheap white paper plates.

We needed a prompt for the children—an idea or topic for them to use when creating their cereal project. We decided on "a new animal at the zoo."

She put samples of cereal on plates, gave each child a plate, put the glue and markers in the center of the table, and turned everyone loose. (I am sure that there was cereal stuck to the ceiling fan and bottom of the dining room table when they were finished.)

The children created their animal using the cereal and markers. They glued the cereal onto the paper plate. Be aware when using this activity with children: They will be very quiet or at times silent during the activity. This is because they are using both sides of the brain.

When the project is complete, the children can show their new animal and tell the others about its wonderful qualities. Older students could write about their new animal. Science students could tell the type of body covering (fur, feathers, scales, etc.), the daily diet, the habitat or biome in which the animals dwell, and so on. Science students could also create a genus and species for this animal. Math students could count the number of toes and then calculate the total toes six new animals would have. I am sure you could come up with a graphing lesson from the data you collect.

You can use any prompt you wish. You can use this any time of the year. Former students tell me that it is a great project for the final day before spring break or any Friday. Prepare in advance on the follow-up you will use—oral expression or written expression. As your follow-up you can take a digital photo of the cereal creation and use that as the basis of future lessons. One could be to compare and contrast three photos of cereal creations. The possibilities are endless.

KWL / KWHL Charts

Donna Ogle (1986) is credited for designing these charts. She first developed the KWL chart in 1986. The KWHL chart was a later design. Your students can invent other variations of this learning standard.

Materials: photocopy paper, magic markers of various colors. Option: a word processor program may be used to create these charts.

KWL stands for "what we *know*," "what we *want* to know," and "what we *learned*." Below is a sample of a KWL chart on the topic of penguins.

KWL chart topic: Penguins
What we know

- Penguins are birds.

What we *want* to know

- How do they stay warm?
- How do they get around?

What we *learned*

- Penguins are great swimmers.

The H section represents "*how* will we learn?" The paper is divided into thirds for a KWL chart and into fourths for a KWHL. Compare the KWL chart with the following KWHL chart on the topic of penguins.

KWHL chart topic: Penguins
What we *know*

- Penguins are birds.

What we *want* to know

- How do they stay warm?
- How do they get around?

How will we find the information?

- Use an encyclopedia.
- Check the Internet; use bookmarked sites.

What we *learned*

- How they stay warm.
- How they get around.

A good way to introduce KWL charts is as a large-group or entire-class project. You can use the chalkboard/whiteboard for this. The teacher would serve as the recorder. A different color can be used for each letter and its corresponding information. After the students become familiar with this process, KWL charts become a good source for student writing and learning. The L section can also be used as an assessment for your chapter or unit. Creative students can devise a new section for the standard KWL chart. One suggestion would be adding an A section that represents "how can we *apply* this information?"

- Summary for administrators: The contents of this chapter provide some creative and innovative ways to teach language arts. When complying with the requirements for the No Child Left Behind Act, incorporate these instructional strategies when preparing for the language arts portion of the standardized test. The students will have learned the material rather than remembering meaningless facts to pass a test.

- Summary for teachers: You can teach the state and national learning standards through these activities. You will be motivated and pumped to come to school each day—as will your children. Pick and choose the language arts activities described throughout this chapter to best meet the learning needs of your students and the learning objectives of your school.
- Summary for homeschool parents: Each of the activities in this chapter utilizes items that you have readily available at home. Select a few activities each week to implement with your child. Then discuss which ones he or she liked best. Continue to implement those activities with your child.
- Summary for community and religious volunteers: Because the activities in this chapter are transferable, you can use them with the learning opportunities you have for the children in your care. They will love the new learning opportunities!

REFERENCES

Farris, P. (2004). *Elementary and middle school social studies: An interdisciplinary, multicultural approach* (4th ed.). Boston: McGraw-Hill.

Ogle, D. (1986). K-W-L: A teaching model that develops active reading of expository text. *The Reading Teacher, 39*, 564–570.

15

MATH

Teaching is not a profession; it is a passion.

—Source unknown

This chapter provides fun, creative, innovative mathematics activities that connect with the three learning styles. Each activity is intended to result in long-term learning or learning². Several mathematical suggestions have already been made in previous chapters, such as using cereal to provide visual and kinesthetic activities for mathematical concepts. Chunking was introduced in the language arts chapter. Chunking will be applied to mathematical principles in this chapter. Turning the notebook paper sideways helps students align their problems as well as distinguish place value. The rainbow spelling technique can be used to distinguish place value. Looped carpet samples and tiles can be used in small-group or learning center activities. The tiles will have numbers as well as mathematical functions ($-$, $\times$, $+$, $=$, and $/$) written on them. Magnetic paint and magnets can be used for activities similar to those used with carpet samples and tiles.

TRIFOLD MULTIPLICATION AND ADDITION
SELF-CHECKING AIDS

Another standard activity that I have used with various grade levels of students is a three-fold math project. I suggest that you use ledger-sized paper—it's two standard 8 1/2 × 11-inch size side by side. Fold the paper in thirds as a "hamburger" fold. The paper will still be 11 inches wide. Use a quarter to draw 8 circles on the top of the trifolded paper. You will have two rows of 4 each. You can also draw 10 circles, two rows of 5 each.

Materials: ledger-sized construction paper, markers or gel pens, scissors.

I used light-colored construction paper for years before the gel pens were invented. Today you can use any color as long as the gel pen shows up.

1. Trace the circles onto the top portion.
2. Cut out the circles.
3. Decorate around the circles. Decide which number family you wish to use for this card. For example, we will choose six. You will write a 6 to the left of each circle. You will randomly write other single-digit numbers to the right of each circle. If you have 8 holes, you can use numbers 2–9 for your numbers to the right. If you have 10 holes, you can use 1–10 or 0–9. You decide.
4. Fold the top portion down so that you can see the second section through the holes. Decide which color you will use to write the answers to each *addition* math problem *inside* the circle. Complete this process. Decide which color you will use to write the answers to each *multiplication* math problem *inside* the circle. Avoid using a red-green combination; students who are colorblind will have trouble distinguishing between these colors.
5. Optional: The card can be laminated at this time, or you may choose to cover it with a clear adhesive coating. If the card is laminated, you will have to cut out the circles once again.

6. Fold the card into thirds. Slip a sheet of notebook paper under the top portion so that the paper shows through the holes. Decide if this will be an *addition* or *multiplication* activity. Then ask the student to complete the problems. They can then open the card and self-check their answers.

I used these in centers with students in grades three through six. They were especially helpful because some of my students in the upper grades had not mastered the basic addition problems. The cards were also helpful for advanced students in third grade who wanted to move ahead of the class learning their multiplication tables.

I suggest that you laminate these cards if at all possible. I brought the sets home one summer—the summer my home was destroyed by an Oklahoma tornado. Those cards withstood the storm and the torrential rains that followed. We found them spread out all over our yard. I wiped them off and returned them to school for several more years of use.

This is a project that parent helpers can do. Students in upper grades can also help create these cards for use with younger students. I do recommend that you check the answers within those circles *before* laminating them. I have had to toss some due to mathematical mistakes made by my helpers.

MAGIC NUMBER

The teacher predetermines the "magic number," writes a large number on photocopy paper, and makes enough copies for the entire class. Depending on the mathematical abilities of the students and the grade level, the students will write math facts that *equal* the magic number. For example, primary students will write addition and subtraction facts that equal the magic number. Upper elementary students can include multiplication and division facts. This concept can also be used with fractions with older students.

As the classroom teacher, you might want to give the students a predetermined minimum of facts that need to be completed. You might even want to give them a specific time frame to complete this task.

Below is a sample of some facts that connect to the magic number of 12.

$$6 + 6 \quad 7 + 5 \quad 12 - 0 \quad 20 - 8 \quad 11 + 1 \quad 3 \times 4$$

As students become proficient in this process, ask the students to get out their own sheets of paper. Ask one student to select the magic number for today. When he or she calls out that number, the other students will write it on their paper and begin the process.

Everyday children are asked to work mundane mathematical problems—and we wonder why they hate math! Math problems always have only one correct answer. This process allows the problems to be divergent. Allowing them to provide divergent answers to math questions allows them creativity and also allows them to think using the inverse process of math. We already know the answer, what is the question? Or in mathematical language, we already know the answer, what is the math problem?

Utilizing the information from previous chapters, allow the students to use colored pencils and markers to add color to this activity. They will retain the information faster and retain it longer with color.

Materials: photocopy paper, pencils, colored pencils, markers.

PLACE VALUE

Many younger students have difficulty with place value. A suggestion to help with this is to use Fruit Loops cereal, which comes in orange, purple, green, red, and blue. You decide which color will represent which place. For example, today purple is 100s, green is 10s, and orange is 1s. You could have this counted out in advance and placed in a snack-size resealable bag. The students will "create" various numbers that you call out. If you say "486," they will show four purple pieces, eight green 10s, and six orange 1s. They can align them in an orderly fashion, align them on notebook paper, or group them on their desk or on a coffee filter. Be sure that the background provides a good contrast for the students to see their manipulatives.

The above example did not include all the colors of Fruit Loops. The two other colors could be used to show decimal places. They could also be used to show 1,000 and 10,000 places to the left of the decimal. You can adjust this activity for the needs of your teaching objective.

Can you use Cheerios? Yes, it is a great example of a manipulative. In the above case, however, the distinction between the colors and the different places of value is vital.

COTTON SWAB GEOMETRY

A fourth math idea involves cotton swabs of any brand. This is a good geometry manipulative and also can be used at a spelling or language arts center for the students to construct "square letters." Square letters are letters two swabs tall. An H would be two swabs tall and one swab wide. An S would be two swabs tall and squared rather than having rounded curves.

Materials: cotton swabs, rubber cement, wax paper, sandwich or snack-size resealable bags, a well-ventilated room—preferably with windows open. Note: This project is to be prepared by the teacher or adult helper rather than the students.

Place the wax paper on a table top or cabinet area. Dip each end of the cotton swab into the rubber cement. Place the cotton swabs on the wax paper and allow them to dry for a few hours or overnight. The ends of the swabs will become tacky and will easily stick to each other. The students can design various geometric shapes as well as 3-D shapes. Again, use a dark background to provide contrast so the students can see their shapes. When they are finished with the cotton swabs, the teacher can collect them and store them for future uses in the resealable bags.

Word of caution: Please do not allow the students to use the rubber cement. Student safety is paramount. Read and follow the cautions on the bottle of rubber cement when preparing this activity.

PLAYING CARDS

A fifth mathematics idea involves playing cards. This is a great learning activity; however, if your principal does not wish for the students to use playing cards for educational purposes, please comply.

Materials: one deck of playing cards, paper (notebook paper turned sideways), and pencil.

Decide in advance the value of the royal cards—the jack, queen, king, and ace. For example, each of these cards could have a value of 1 or a value or 10. If the decision is not made in advance, much confusion occurs. The students select a certain number of cards and create a column addition problem. They align the cards on a desk and then write the problem on their notebook paper, which is running sideways to provide them with straight lines. They then complete the column addition problem and select more cards. This could be set up at a center, and the students could use a calculator for self-checking.

Aside from column addition, multidigit addition, subtraction, multiplication, and division problems can be constructed in this way. The advantage of using playing cards is that you are continuously getting new numbers with which to work.

DOMINOS

Another mathematics activity is very similar to the example above. This activity involves dominos. Before starting this project, remove any dominos that have a total larger than the value of 10.

Materials: one set of dominos, paper (notebook paper turned sideways), and pencil.

The students turn the dominos face down, blank side up. They select a specified number of dominos and create a column addition problem. The students then write down their problem on the paper (running sideways) and calculate the answer.

Students can turn the dominos sideways to create a two-digit addition problem. Again, this can become a multiplication, subtraction, or division problem. It is a good center activity. This project also works well when you have multiple levels of learners in your math group.

Many mathematics books have a reproducible domino page. Photocopy this onto cardstock so that one side won't show through to the other side. You can then cut out your dominos and place them in resealable bags for storage. This would be a good project to laminate if you have that option available.

LEARNING MULTIPLICATION FACTS

One mathematics suggestion examines the topic of chunking, as previously discussed. According to Kellough (1996), students need to learn only 36 multiplication facts when you eliminate the identity property, the multiply-by-zero or zero property, and the commutative property. Remember that multiplication and division are the reverse of each other, just as addition and subtraction are. You teach the identity property when you teach students that any number multiplied by 1 is the same number (example: $1 \times 946 = 946$). We teach the zero property when we tell them that any number multiplied by 0 is 0 (example, $0 \times 946 = 0$). The commutative property is best taught orally. Read the following mathematical information out loud, and you will understand.

$6 \times 4 = 24$
$4 \times 6 = 24$

You have just switched the first two numbers. They still provide the same answer.

So after these three necessities have been taught, the students need to learn only 36 separate multiplication facts. Among these 36 facts lurk the walk-in-the-park facts of the 2s and the 5s. That shrinks our 36 total to only 16 facts. Wow! That is an attainable number. When you teach division, it is the reverse operation of multiplication. For example, 35 divided by 7 can be transposed to ask "What do we multiply 7 by to get 35?" Bingo! We know our multiplication tables, so we know the answer!

TILE SPACERS

An inexpensive manipulative found at hardware stores can be used to show mathematical functions ($-$, $\times$, $+$, $=$, and $/$). I first noticed students using bags of tile spacers at the eighth grade level to demonstrate positive and negative numbers. I was so happy to see students at this grade level using math manipulatives. As the students worked at their desks, the teacher modeled the procedure using an overhead machine. The tile spacers make an $\times$ or a $+$, whichever way they are placed on the background. The classroom teacher had trimmed some of the spacers to become $-$ signs as well as using whole spacers to represent $+$ signs. Each student counted out the number of $+$ manipulatives to represent the number of positive numbers. Directly below those manipulatives, they counted out the number of $-$, negative numbers. (I would have used notebook paper running sideways for the background.) They could easily see the extra number of manipulatives left over—the answer to the problem.

Materials: one package of tile spacers, old pair of scissors to trim the spacers, resealable bags to hold the manipulatives.

If tile spacers can be used to represent positive and negative numbers, what other ways can they be used? As classroom teachers, we are slow to toss away anything. What if we saved the leftover pieces that were trimmed away to make the $+$ and $-$? What could we do with the leftovers? Those pieces could be trimmed to represent the dots that go on top of and below the line to show a division sign. The + to show positive or addition could be turned slightly to represent × —the multiplication sign. And, most brilliantly, two subtraction signs could be placed one on top of the other to represent an = sign. Every mathematical function can be created from these rubbery inexpensive tile spacers.

I used these function symbols with numbers that were cut out of craft foam. I bought them in a huge tub at a craft store. These can be made using an Ellison machine. You could also use letters cut from construction paper or card stock. You could use the ceramic or purchased tiles I have previously mentioned. This could be a small-group or learning center activity. Be sure the background has a good contrast. Most tile spacers are light in color.

BENDABLE STRAWS

This is an inexpensive kinesthetic and visual activity for primary students learning various geometric shapes. There are two types of straws. You want to use the straws that have the bendable section near one end.

Materials: bendable straws, background that provides a good contrast for students.

This activity could be part of a learning center or part of an individual activity. It really doesn't work well as a large group project because everyone wants to participate at once.

If you want the students to create or replicate a square, they will need four bendable straws. One tip is very helpful: Always pinch the same end of the straw. For example, tell the students to always pinch the end closest to the bendable end. That way things will fit together much better. Ask the students to pinch the end closest to the bendable end and slip it into the end of a second straw that is farthest from the bendable end. Continue this process until all four straws are connected. Voila! We have a square that can be lifted and examined, hung from the ceiling, placed on a bulletin board, or kept flat on the desk. This activity appeals to the auditory learner when they discuss their shape or name other items that are this shape.

The same process can be used with three or more straws. The geometric figures can be taken apart and stored in a resealable bag or bundled up with a rubber band and saved for another day of learning. This is a great filler activity when an assembly is cancelled or you have some unanticipated extra time during your day.

MARDI GRAS BEADS

This is a colorful way to teach students about grouping or multiplication. There are two types of Mardi Gras beads. One type is continuous, and if you cut the string, they will all come apart. The other type is knotted so that if you cut the string, the beads will still stay on the string. You want to buy this type.

Materials: Mardi Gras strands of beads of various colors, resealable bag for storage for each set.

Using one colored strand, select your number. If you are going to set up a set to demonstrate the nines, you will cut the beads so that you have strands of nine beads per strand. Place your set of nines in a resealable bag. You would use a different color to create a set of sixes, a different color for a set of fours, and so forth. Once you create these sets, they will be used year after year with your students.

To use the sets, if the math problem was 9×4, the students would select nine sets with four beads per strand. To show transferability, they could also select four sets with nine beads per strand. The color used for the nines would be different from the color used for the fours. This project could be completed in a large group, small group, or learning center setting.

MATH

MULTIPLICATION GLOVES

You can purchase plastic or rubber gloves at a low cost. Often they are sold in multiple sets. You can also use white cotton gloves found at hardware or gardening stores. Note: Some students are allergic to latex gloves. Because you are preparing the sets of gloves to be used year after year with students, avoid using latex gloves for this project. Student safety is paramount.

Materials: one set of plastic or white cotton gloves, permanent marker, and a resealable bag for storage.

Every time I start to make these, I toss the first pair in the trash. There is a tip to creating this learning activity. Lay the gloves on a desk facing *palm up*, with pinkie fingers in the middle; that way, when the students are wearing the gloves and looking at them the numbers will be in the right sequence. Just as the Mardi Gras beads were divided into sets, each pair of gloves will be one set. For illustration, write a large 3 on the palm of each glove. Beginning on the thumb of the left glove, write a 0 with a permanent marker. The index finger will have a 1, and so forth. On the right glove, write a 5 on the pinkie finger and proceed. The thumb of the right glove will have 9 written on it.

Now comes the tricky part. With the gloves still facing you, fold down the fingernail portion of the gloves. Here is where you will write the answer to each problem, but you will write it so that the numbers can be seen while you are wearing the gloves and bending your fingers to see the answers. Don't write them upside down! The thumb of the left glove will have 0 written for the answer to the problem $3 \times 0 = 0$. The index finger will have 3 written on the folded-down portion, and so forth.

This is a self-checking activity for students. The gloves can be kept in a resealable bag with the proper number written on it in permanent marker. The students can "feel" the multiplication as they bend their fingers, they can see the problems (especially if colored permanent markers are used), and they can say the process as it evolves; thus, it involves all three learning styles. One suggestion for the teacher: The students' hands will sweat if they wear these gloves very long. You might want to set a guideline that they use one set and then watch their partners go through the process.

DROP OF WATER

This process was discussed in the language arts chapter. We will now examine its use in mathematics and social studies. You can show magnification in science by placing a drop of water on a sheet of wax paper that is on top of a piece of newspaper. The students are always amazed at the power of this drop of water.

For math, use a sheet of notebook paper or a paper towel, and place a penny on top. The penny needs to be tails up. By placing a drop of water on top of the penny, the students can see Abraham Lincoln *inside* the Lincoln Memorial. If you take the pennies out into the sunlight, they can see a small speck inside the Memorial.

Another fun activity involves prediction and verification. The students predict how many drops of water will "stand" on the penny, as opposed to running off. They then use the straw eyedropper (discussed in the language arts chapter) to verify their answer. I have placed some pennies in the freezer overnight to have the variable of temperature added to this activity. I have also asked the students to place the penny in their pocket or hand for a while prior to the activity. Again, the variable of temperature is added to the procedure. I always ask the students to write down their predictions and then write down the actual number of drops the penny holds. You can graph both sets of information. You can also graph the difference—the difference between the guessed number and the actual number.

You can also draw various geometric shapes of varying sizes on a paper and photocopy it for the entire class. Be sure to place a dot on each shape. This dot will represent the starting point.

Using wax paper and a toothpick, place a drop of water on the wax paper. The students drag the water to the starting point. They then "race" the water around the shape till they return to the dot again. This can be timed—and the results graphed. A drop or two of food coloring to the water adds the element of color to this activity.

You can use this same process in social studies with maps. The students can trace around the various states or countries. They can trace the Mississippi River from Minnesota to the Gulf of Mexico. They can outline continents using a drop of water. The teacher can color the water green for the students to trace the Nile River in Africa.

- Summary for administrators: Math is a major component of No Child Left Behind. The instructional strategies in this chapter help upper elementary students benefit from the kinesthetic learning opportunities generally used only by primary students. The strategies encompass the spectrum of learning styles. A great alternative to worksheets and paper and pencil math lessons!

  I encourage you to take one of the instructional strategies from this chapter and implement it in your office. Put on a pair of multiplication gloves. Get out a sheet of paper and create your own magic number. Take a penny out of your pocket and look for Mr. Lincoln. You will enjoy the process and learn. So will children in their classrooms.
- Summary for teachers: According to the statistics from Sousa (1998) in previous chapters, your classroom will consist of 46 percent visual learners, 35 percent kinesthetic learners, and 19 percent auditory learners. The instructional strategies in this chapter appeal to all three learning styles—100 percent. Rather than using paper and pencil to complete math problems, get out the manipulatives and learn! No more math phobia in your classroom!
- Summary for homeschool parents: Your child will benefit from the instructional strategies that appeal to all learning styles. Get out the cotton swabs, gloves, and dominos, and watch your child learn and love math!
- Summary for community and religious volunteers: Practice that drop of water activity with the penny. You will be able to

see Lincoln in the Memorial. Pick and choose from the creative activities in this chapter to best meet the needs of the children in your care.

REFERENCES

Kellough, R. D. (1996.) *Integrating mathematics and science for intermediate and middle school students.* Englewood Cliffs, NJ: Merrill/Prentice Hall.

Sousa, D. (1998). *How the brain learns: More new insights for educators.* A presentation on August 18, 1998, Port Washington, WI.

16

SCIENCE AND SOCIAL STUDIES

My heart is singing for joy this morning. A miracle has happened! The light of understanding has shown upon my little pupil's mind, and behold, all things are changed.

—Anne Sullivan

I have been teaching subjects in an integrated curricular approach since 1975. I am always taking an integrated approach to learning. Science and social studies are so easy to combine, along with language arts and mathematics. In this chapter the reader will find ideas that can easily transfer into all curricular areas as well as utilizing at least two of the learning styles with each activity. Each of the student activities within this chapter are intended to produce long-term learning or learning[2].

MNEMONICS

When this word is pronounced, the first *m* is silent. This memory aid dates back to the ancient Greeks. The word *mnemonic* comes from the Greek word *mnema*, which means "memory."

Mnemonics have been part of our learning process for most of our lives. We just didn't know the term. Remember the social studies jingle

"In 1492 Columbus sailed the ocean blue"? That was a mnemonic. A simple Internet search will bring up many sites that have hundreds of mnemonics in many categories. For example, "**E**at **An As**pirin **Af**ter **A Na**ff **Sa**ndwich" represents the continents of **E**urope, **An**tarctica, **As**ia, **Af**rica, **A**ustralia, **N. A**merica, **S. A**merica (*The Continents*, 2000). "Kids prefer cheese over fried green spinach" is a mnemonic for the proper ordering of biological groupings—kingdom, phylum, class, order, family, genus, and species (Hargis, n.d.).

Some mnemonics are poems rather than phrases. Here is an example of the parts of speech (*The Parts of Speech*, 1997). The creative teacher would add movements to the recitation of this poem to involve the kinesthetic learner.

"Every name is called a NOUN,
As *field* and *fountain*, *street* and *town*;
In place of noun the PRONOUN stands,
As *he* and *she* can clap their hands;
The ADJECTIVE describes a thing,
As *magic* wand and *bridal* ring;
The VERB means action, something done—
To *read* and *write*, to *jump* and *run*;
How things are done, the ADVERBS tell,
As *quickly, slowly, badly, well*;
The PREPOSITION shows relation,
As *in* the street, or *at* the station;
CONJUNCTIONS join, in many ways,
Sentences, words, *or* phrase *and* phrase;
The INTERJECTION cries out, '*Hark!*
I need an exclamation mark!'
Through Poetry, we learn how each
of these make up the PARTS OF SPEECH."

Our brains need to connect with something for long-term knowledge to be stored—as learned information. There are times when this is just not possible. That's when the teacher can use mnemonic strategies to help the learning process. According to Wolfe (2002), a mnemonic

> creates links or associations that give the brain an organizational framework on which to hook new information. The process is relatively simple and consists of three basic steps:
>
> The student has—or is given—a framework.
> New items are associated with the framework.
> The known cues—the framework—aid in the recall of the new information. (pp. 179–180)

If mnemonics have been used since the time of the ancient Greeks, they have staying power. Based on your subject matter, begin your search today for mnemonics that can be utilized in your classroom. Also consider having a class project in which the students help create new mnemonics. The options are endless. This activity appeals to the auditory learner. When color is added to writing the mnemonic, the visual and kinesthetic learners are involved.

STATES, STATE CAPITOLS, STATE HISTORY

At the elementary level, a social studies national curriculum standard includes the study of state history. Many state curriculum standards also include the requirement of naming the states and capitols. When I was a child, we loved to check the license plates on the cars that drove up Main Street in Collinsville, Oklahoma. It was such a thrill to find a car with out-of-state plates. This was also a favorite pastime for families taking a road trip.

A fun substitute for the license plates is to look in our pockets or pocketbooks. The U. S. Mint has provided educators with a great resource—the state quarters and the Westward Journey nickels. The mint also provides individuals with Internet access to a plethora of resources on these coins. Teachers and parents can print out history and information about the symbols on each coin. You can place this information at a learning station or use it with a small group. See *A Celebration of the 50 States* (U.S Mint, 2006) and *2005 Westward Journey Nickel Series* (U.S. Mint, 2005). Use these references to design kinesthetic learning activities for your students. Many of the images show historical sites or individuals. Aside from history, the coin series leads to discussions on economics. You could design the Who, What? When? Where? Why? How much? How many? questions around a story of these coins. The interrogative cards discussed in an earlier chapter could be used. These coins provide endless activities for students.

A second resource for studying the states, capitols, and state history is using books from the Sleeping Bear Press, Discover America State by State Series. These are alphabet books written in verse or lyric form. For example, the book about Oklahoma's history is *S is for Sooner*. You will have to search for your state book. The website (www.sleepingbearpress.com) offers parents and teachers educational resources for each book. I checked the site for information about *Penny: the Forgotten Coin* and found a teacher's guide consisting of 22 pages of fun activities for children. Each book has similar resources. You can go to www.sleepingbearpress.com or contact them by phone at 1-800-487-2323. The public library system as well as the school library would be helpful in locating these books.

CHAINS

Chains were discussed in the language arts chapter. Consider using chains to write the vocabulary words and definitions from science and social studies. Also consider using chains to construct food chains. The links can be color codes so that the herbivores are written on green links, the carnivores are written on red links, and so on. I found that the students just did not understand the concept of the food chain. I whipped out paper and started linking the various categories together. I could see their brains going into overdrive making connections.

CLASSIFICATION OF ANIMALS

This can be the most boring concept ever to teach! Consider making this relevant to the students. We used the mascots for the NFL football teams that were animals. We then had our animals; we just had to find the genus and species for each animal. (We could have found more information, but we were elementary students.) This activity makes a dull topic relevant to students. You could take this activity a step further and locate the biomes or habitats in which these animals dwell. A final step would be to construct a food chain involving this animal. What a fun science project to start off the school year—it will be football season and the students will be saturated with NFL games on television. Aside from the NFL teams, you could use your school mascot if it is an animal. Lion, tigers, and bears—oh my!

Bears are a super topic for an integrated curricular study. A study of the classification of animals will show that pandas are not part of the bear family. I used to bring in my entire bear collection in my university science class. Each student researched a bear. They were told the genus of the bear, but they decided the species. My teacher bear might be named *ursa teacher*. My Smokey the Bear might be titled *ursa ranger*. This then led to a writing project in which the student wrote a rationale for their choice of bear name. They included the habitat or biome in which this particular bear lived. The list of possibilities was endless for this project.

We also discussed the possibility of elementary students having a teddy bear picnic. (For song lyrics, see *Words to the Teddy Bear's Picnic Song* [n.d.]. For picnic ideas, see #306. *Teddy Bear Picnic* [n.d.]) They can bring something sweet or something salty from home in a resealable bag. Put the sweet food items in a large bowl and mix them. Then use a cup to fill small resealable bags for the students to have trail mix or picnic mix. The same process is involved with salty foods. With any food project, be sure to avoid any items your students might be allergic to. We used to make "whale watching mix" during our integrated study of whales and the ocean. Community volunteers and religious teachers can use this activity to correspond to your studies easily.

CASH REGISTER TAPE

Cash register tape comes in a variety of widths. You decide which size is best for your students. One roll will last a very long time. I always precut my tape and had it ready to pass out at the beginning of the project, as opposed to standing and cutting during class time.

For my sixth grade language arts students, we used five sections to draw the five most important events from the life of our biography source. We would then add a narrative on the sections. We put them together in a comic book format. We also used a similar format in my university art class to create a comic strip from our thumbprints.

Science students can use cash register tape to record their observations of the phases of the moon. They can go out each evening, make observations, and then draw or write a written description of their observations. This is an at-home project. (Parents or caregivers need to be with the children outside.) Students should write the date of each observation on the strip.

I have seen a similar project using cash register tape with middle school science students. A circle cutter was used to cut white and black circles. The students then overlapped the circles to show the various phases of the moon. They glued the shapes onto the cash register tape in sequence.

Cash register tape is also a great way to show sequence in various historical events. Students can write in the various information to make time lines. These sections can be combined to make bulletin boards.

RESEALABLE BAGS

I have suggested using resealable bags throughout the chapters of this book. Resealable bags can also be used as the focus of learning activities for students.

Classroom teachers can create a class terrarium using a gallon-sized bag. There are also resealable bags that have special bottoms that stand alone. This type would also be good for terrariums. When the bag is sealed, the terrarium becomes its own ecosystem. Because the bag is clear, the students can make observations.

The same size bag can be used to create a classroom aquarium. Fill the bottom with aquarium gravel. Follow expert advice about aging and adding water and fish that would be appropriate for this type of aquarium.

Slime is a favorite project of students of all ages. You can find a plethora of slime recipes on the Internet. Food coloring can be added to color your slime. The beauty of using resealable bags is that the preparation of slime is no-mess because the entire recipe can be completed inside the bag, then tossed away for easy cleanup. I have used colored slime as a prompt for creative writing activities. I have also used the corn starch and water recipe to show students the three states of matter. When the slime is held in the palm of students' hands, it turns from a solid into a liquid. When it drops onto a surface, it transforms back into a solid again.

Cooking projects can be mixed in resealable bags. There are many no-bake cooking recipes that are great for classrooms. The entire process of no-bake recipes could be done inside resealable bags. I helped a first grade class make pumpkin pudding one autumn. We used plastic cups, but resealable bags would have worked well also. Check your recipes and also check online for recipes that could be made inside a resealable bag.

VENN DIAGRAMS

Venn diagrams were named after the originator, John Venn, who developed this method of comparing and contrasting in 1880 in England. In mathematics, Venn diagrams can be used to show relationships between sets. In language arts, Venn diagrams can be used to show similarities and differences between characters, stories, poems, and so on. When introducing Venn diagrams to your students, consider doing this as a group project in which you guide the class through the process. When the students become familiar with the diagrams, they can then branch out into creating these as a small-group or independent project. You can use Venn diagrams in any curricular area as well as with any age group. Color can enhance learning.

Venn diagrams are traditionally considered to be two overlapping circles or ovals. Two sources are contrasted on the far left and far right sections. They are compared for similarities in the center section. The teacher can provide the students with diagrams on photocopy paper. The class can also vary from the traditional circles and use two shapes that are related to the subject. In figure 16.1, the students will compare and contrast a circle and a square. Any two shapes can be used.

You can create the shapes for Venn diagrams using Microsoft Word. Please follow the steps carefully.

1. Open Word. Go to Insert, Picture, Autoshapes.
2. Select a circle or oval. Play with the size until you have the size you desire.

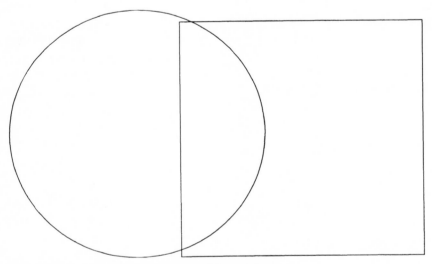

Figure 16.1.   Venn diagram using two different shapes

3. With the boxes around the shape, go to Edit, Copy.
4. You will now Paste this shape onto the page. Adjust the shape so that it overlaps the present shape you have.
5. Now right-click on Format, Autoshapes. Left-click under the topic No Fill under the Fill (color) category at the top. Then select OK. This will make the circle continue its shape.
6. To make three or more shapes for your Venn Diagram, continue step 5 as many times as you wish.
7. To create text within your Venn diagram, follow the steps below.
8. Go to Insert, Textbox. Place the textbox in the desired location.
9. Type the text in the box.
10. With the boxes selected, go to Format, Textbox. Left-click on Line, Color, No Line, OK. Your lines for the textbox will be erased.

Venn diagrams can be made out of inexpensive paper plates. The students cut along the ribbed section of two plates. They then use a brad to hold both plates together. When the paper plate Venn diagrams are placed on top of notebook paper or photocopy paper, the students can write the information on the paper.

Two hula hoops can be placed on the tray of the whiteboard or chalkboard. These hoops will form the framework for a huge Venn diagram. Hula hoops can also be placed on the blacktop area of the playground or on the concrete on the sidewalk to show the same principle. When you use Venn diagrams in the ways mentioned, they provide enriched learning opportunities for the auditory, visual, and kinesthetic learners.

CONCEPT MAPS

The final teaching strategy suggestion in this chapter is concept maps or concept webs. They provide visual, kinesthetic, and auditory experiences for learners. When introducing this information to your class, use an entire-class approach. As the students become more familiar with the concept, they can branch out and create their own maps or webs. Encourage them to add various color and shapes to their maps. Teachers can also use concept maps as a unit or chapter assessment for any curricular area.

Students organize their thoughts in written form. The general procedure is to have students identify important concepts in the content that is being studied. The students then rank-order or prioritize the concepts from the most general to the most specific. The final step is to arrange the concepts on a page, connect the related ideas with lines, and define the connections between the related ideas. This will provide a visual relationship or interconnectedness between the figures and the central theme.

Concept maps begin with a central shape. Other figures branch out from the center and are also connected back to the center. Encourage your students to write the topic of the map inside the center shape and the various components inside the other figures. Figure 16.2 shows an example of a concept map.

The simplest basis for a concept map is Why? What? When? Where? Who? How many/How much? The theme would be written in the center shape. The Ws and Hs would be the next shapes. The subsequent shapes would contain the answers to the above questions.

- Summary for administrators: This chapter offers a myriad of instructional strategies that are transferable—they can be used with basically any curricular area. Recall the quote from the introduction by Roger Lewin (as cited in *Hoagie's Gifted Education*, 2006): "Too often we give children answers to remember rather than problems to solve." This chapter has provided the reader with creative, innovative problem-solving activities for children. The concepts described in this chapter, as well as throughout the book, go beyond filling in the blanks—or as Lewin states "giving children answers to remember."

  As the administrator of your school site, do you want classrooms filled with students who are given answers to remember or provided with innovative, creative problem-solving activities? Please provide the supplies for your faculty to stretch be-

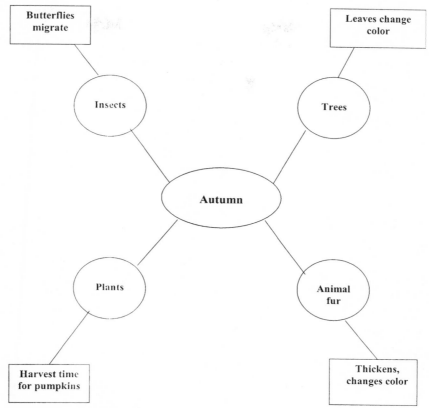

Figure 16.2. Concept map

yond the boundaries of basic regurgitation to learning[2]. The choice is yours.

• Summary for teachers: The strategies in this chapter are transferable—they can be adapted to virtually any curricular area. Your students will learn from creating concept maps and Venn diagrams. These activities—as well as the others in the chapter—will make the students think. According to Albert Schweitzer, "The most important goal of education is to make young people think for themselves." Use mnemonics to their fullest potential. Get out strips of paper and help your students make learning chains. Remember the passion of teaching and learning!

- Summary for homeschool parents: You can find great learning opportunities for your child in this chapter. Utilize them with your child. These instructional strategies, along with the others in this book, appeal to all three learning styles.
- Summary for community and religious volunteers: Whatever the concept you are trying to teach your students, you can utilize some activities from this chapter to help your students learn. You will enjoy teaching. They will enjoy learning!

REFERENCES

#306. Teddy Bear Picnic. (n.d.). Retrieved April 10, 2006, from www.teachers.net/lessons/posts/306.html.

The continents. (2000). Retrieved from www.eudesign.com/mnems/_mnframe.htm.

Hargis, A. (n.d.). *Mnemonics: Biology.* Retrieved from http://users.frii.com/geomanda/mnemonics/biology.html.

Hoagie's gifted education: Education quotes. (2006). Retrieved from www.hoagiesgifted.org/education_quotes.htm.

The parts of speech. (1997). Retrieved from www.eudesign.com/mnems/_mnframe.htm.

U.S. Mint. (2005). *2005 Westward Journey Nickel Series.* Retrieved April 10, 2006, from www.usmint.gov/mint_programs/index.cfm?action=nickel_series.

U.S. Mint. (2006). *A celebration of the 50 states.* Retrieved April 10, 2006, from www.usmint.gov/mint_programs/index.cfm?action=50_state_quarters_program.

Wolfe, P. (2002). *Brain matters: Translating research into classroom practice.* Alexandria, VA: Association of Supervision and Curriculum Development.

Words to the Teddy Bear's Picnic Song. (n.d.). Retrieved April 10, 2006, from www.dltk-kids.com/crafts/teddy/teddypicnic.html.

ASSESSMENT
AND EVALUATION

17

DID THEY LEARN?

When someone is taught the joy of learning it becomes a life-long process that never stops, a process that creates a logical individual. That is the challenge and joy of teaching.

—Marva Collins

Teach as though you were teaching your own children.

—Anonymous

Teach as though you were teaching your own grandchildren.

—Dr. Linda Henshall Wilson

This book has covered everything from improving learning, knowing the times we learn best, creating and maintaining an enriched learning environment, including music in the classroom, and a zillion creative learning opportunities for children—all with the intention of promoting long-term learning for students or learning[2]. After you put the information from this book into practice, how will you know if they have learned it? This chapter takes on that question and answers it with the most recent examples of assessments and evaluations.

Before beginning a weight loss program, you must first take that dreaded step of getting on the scales and learning your current weight. You will then be able to track your progress. The same is true of student learning. You have set objectives and a plan or agenda for the lesson using the contents of chapter 13. Now, working with that all-important teaching or learning objective, you must create a tool to measure student learning. You can set this evaluation instrument up so that it reflects a percentage number that you can enter in the grade book. (I realize that the readership of this book is varied, and some of you may not need to tabulate or calculate a percentage.)

A step of the teaching process that is too often overlooked is reflection. We simply do not have the time. When we do reflect, we need to take a long look at student grades to see how they are doing and how we are helping in that process.

THE STEPS OF ASSESSMENT

Here are some suggestions for assessments and evaluations.

- Determine the purpose of the assessment.
- What type of test format will best evaluate how students met the objectives? Your assessment needs to be age appropriate and developmentally appropriate. You cannot give first graders an essay test!
- Assemble the assessment with the focus on your objectives through the unit or chapter.
- Administer the assessment. Provide a quiet testing environment for all students. Be sure to tell them in advance what they are to do when they finish the test.
- Evaluate the assessment.
- Reflect on the results.
- Record the results. I realize that, due to the broad intended readership, some of you will not be recording test results.
- Analyze and reflect on the results both collectively and individually in order to improve instruction and, thus, learning.

PRE- AND POSTTESTS

An easy way to determine if student learning has indeed occurred is to conduct pre- and posttests. Basically, you take the same examination and administer it at the beginning of a chapter or unit. You score the students' papers. When instruction has concluded at the end of instruction, you administer the same examination again. You then compare and contrast the student scores. What was the average or mean score of the first examination? What was the mean score of the second examination? How much did the scores vary? The students should have failed the first test. To see that long-term learning or learning[2] occurred, they should have done much better the second time. One suggestion: If you have a student who is absent for the first examination, administer it the day he or she returns. You can still include that score to calculate the group average. Again, if any students are absent on the day of the second test, provide a time for them to make up the examination. Then calculate their scores with the groups' to find the average or mean score.

Some textbook series will provide the teachers with an end-of-the-chapter test. This could be the basis of your pre- and posttests. Most math books have an end-of-the-year test. You would need to get the test from the previous year to administer at the beginning of the year. Then follow up with the end-of-the-year test from your book. For example, if you are teaching fourth grade math, use the end-of-the-year test from third grade for your pretest and the end of the year test from the fourth grade book for your posttest. You can group the questions and run an average on just the addition questions or just the story problems. That breakdown of information will be helpful to you for diagnostic purposes throughout the year.

FORMATIVE VERSUS SUMMATIVE

Formative assessment includes daily assignments, quizzes, or practice tests. The teacher instantly knows if the student knows the material.

The key to formative assessment is up-to-date grading. If you wait days to grade papers, the students may have continued to make systematic errors. By keeping up with grading, you can catch any problems and nip them in the bud.

Summative assessment includes chapter tests or end-of-the-quarter or end-of-the-semester tests. These are a summation of learned information and content covering specified material. After your class has finished studying rocks, give a summative test. Then put your file and teaching materials about rocks back in the file cabinet till next year. The test you gave was a summation of the rock unit.

TYPES OF QUESTIONS

There are various types of test questions. The easiest to describe are the *supply* and *select* questions. When students supply the answer to a question, they respond to a supply question. When students select the answer from a group of choices, they respond to a select question. Select questions include multiple-choice questions, true-false questions, and matching questions. Note: Supply questions are easy to construct but take much longer to grade. Select questions can be considered objective in nature. There is no room for discussion about a question being partially correct.

Convergent questions are lower level questions, basic recall. These questions are at the lower end of Bloom's Taxonomy. There is only one correct answer. For example, for the question "Who was the first president of the United States?" there is obviously only one answer that would be considered correct.

Divergent questions have more than one correct answer. Some children rarely get to work with these types of questions. Divergent questions involve higher order thinking skills—and are more difficult to grade for the teacher, who must know *all* the correct answers. Divergent questions are at the upper end of Bloom's Taxonomy. For example, after studying a unit on the presidents in February, a question might be "Which president do you believe was the best leader for our country and why?" The can of worms has been opened, and they are crawling everywhere. The teacher grading this question must be looking for a president's name and also the rationale for the selection. It is very different from the George Washington question in the previous paragraph.

PERFORMANCE TESTS

Due to the wide variety of curricular areas students encounter, they will be asked to take performance tests in which they perform a task. This might be playing a musical instrument, giving a speech, singing the scale, or writing an essay. Performance tests are graded subjectively. They are based on the teacher's opinion.

WHO GRADES THE WORK?

In today's classrooms an evaluation instrument can be developed that allows the student (self), a peer, and the teacher to assess the student's work. This gives excellent feedback to the student. The instrument can be designed so that the peer grades a paper and does not know the source. This is a great idea because it allows the peer to see another example of work and also maintains the confidentiality of the author. Also, an author reviewing the peer-graded work is also in the dark about which peer graded the paper or project. There is anonymity on both sides. Peer grading or peer reviews are intended to be a learning process for everyone. Abraham Maslow once said, "We learn from the experiences of others." This is surely true of peer grading.

Why do students need to grade their own papers? When the teacher provides a rubric, checklist, or rating scale for the students, all the required information is included. A self-check allows the students to review exactly what is required and see if they have completed everything.

Obviously, the classroom teacher is also responsible for grading student work. Including a self-graded assessment and also a peer-graded assessment—even occasionally—provides a good composite of the student's strengths and weaknesses. Three potential pitfalls to avoid are (1) grading too harshly, (2) grading too easily, and (3) giving an across-the-board grade. The "Grinch syndrome" is giving every student low grades. If the Grinch were grading papers, I am sure he would take this approach. The "middle-of-the-road syndrome" is giving everyone the same grade. Students are not all the same in ability and performance. The "Santa Claus syndrome" is giving everyone a good grade. If Santa were grading papers, I am sure he would be very generous with the grades. Grade objectively. I am required to check the grade books of the first-year teachers I supervise. I always check to see if they are recording grades and also how the students are doing academically. I generally see very high grades on weekly spelling examinations. Sometimes I see a student with a string of zeros and I will ask the reason. Perhaps the student has been absent for several days. If he or she is present and not producing, we have a problem. I also check to see if one of the "syndromes" is prevalent in the grading scheme. If everyone is making a near perfect score or if everyone is failing, we have a Santa or Grinch grading the papers in this room.

CHECKLISTS

The purpose of a checklist is to answer the question of "yes" or "no"—to analyze. A checklist is a set of written criteria in which the teacher, peer, or student determines "yes" or "no." Checklists have only two choices. A checklist does not give a total composite of the student's abilities. Checklists are considered to be objective. The criterion is either met or not met. There is no gray area. True-false questions are also objective. The answer is either true or false. Multiple-choice questions are also objective. If the correct answer is D, then the student either chose D as correct or did not. This clear-cut, black-or-white approach is objective. Subjective grading brings shades of gray into the grading criteria. Suggestion: When using checklists, rating scales, and rubrics with students, *always* give the students the grading instrument *before* they complete the assignment. As educators, we rarely get to use the term *always*. Use this practice with each evaluation.

Checklists provide documentation of projects and performance tasks. Often checklists are used along with portfolios. The checklist provides the framework for the contents of the portfolio. Checklists can be used with a variety of age groups and can also be constructed as peer checklists, student checklists, and the teacher's checklist. Again, you will have multiple sources of an evaluation. Primary and preschool teachers use checklists to document if (and also when) a student meets a curricular goal, such as "recites the alphabet."

Chapter 14 introduced the reader to the KWL charts. Revisiting the KWL chart on the topic of penguins, the teacher can create a checklist based on the students' work.

You can check to see if the requirements were met by using the KWL chart checklist. Please note that this checklist allows checking by the student, peer, and teacher. It also has a space to check so that the group can be documented. There is a space to write in the date that the checklist was assessed and also the date that the student completed the work.

Please refer to Appendix A for a sample of the checklist and steps to create it.

RATING SCALES

Rating scales provide a better level of assessment of the student's work than do checklists. Rating scales look at the performance in terms of degree rather than just "yes" or "no" from the checklist. Checklists are considered objective because the criterion is either met or not. There is no gray area. Rating scales are subjective. They rely on the judgment of the teacher or individual rating the performance of the student. Rating scales are used with several degrees of proficiency, such as *needs to improve, good,* and *excellent;* or *needs to improve, acceptable,* and *target.* Rating scales that use these descriptions are referred to as *descriptive rating scales.* Suggestion: When using rating scales, along with checklists and rubrics, always give the students the evaluation instrument *prior* to the assignment. By taking the time to put the criteria in writing and going over them with students *prior* to the assignment, you will do a better job of explaining the criteria to the students. This is a great example of a win-win situation. Appendix B gives an example of a descriptive rating scale.

When you work with younger children, they often respond well to visuals or graphics rather than written descriptions. There is a rating scale that provides the graphics for children—the graphic rating scale. You can easily distinguish it from the others because it uses symbols to visually show the children's progress. Appendix C takes the same information from appendix B but uses graphic visuals rather than numbers.

Rating scales are useful with all performance learning opportunities. They have the same criteria for every student—the objective from the lesson. Rating scales can be assigned a number value and, thus, can be recorded in the grade book. We refer to this type of rating scale as a numerical rating scale. One suggestion when using numerical rating scales: Before creating the rating scale, calculate the total point value. You can then divide by the number of criteria you have and get the number of points per criterion. Too often teacher education candidates will design a lesson, and the total point value is only 6 or 8 points. Trying to maintain a high level of student motivation is always a goal of teachers. Set your total point value higher so that you can help to keep student motivation on the ceiling. Appendix D provides an example of a numerical rating scale.

Both the graphic and numerical rating scales can be adapted for self or peer reviews. Appendix E shows the heading portion of a rating scale that can be used by the teacher, a peer, or a student. The individual grading the work simply checks the appropriate box, signs, and dates the instrument. Note: You could design it so that the peer does not give his or her name to preserve anonymity.

Many readers are probably asking, "If you can use graphics with a rating scale, why can't you use graphics with a checklist?" A graphic checklist has not yet been invented—until now. I think this would be a great idea to use with learners of any age. It would certainly appeal to the visual learner. With so many preschool and kindergarten programs utilizing checklists now, this would be a good method for a teacher check or self-check on portfolios for younger students. Appendix F shows a graphic checklist I created.

RUBRICS

Rubrics are used to take a performance task and assign a number grade to record the project or performance in the grade book. There are three types of rubrics—holistic, analytical, and scoring. This book focuses on the scoring rubric, which theoretically can be considered a descriptive rating scale (see the previous section). To review, checklists tell the evaluator "yes" or "no." Rating scales can detect degrees of student performance. Rubrics can assign a numerical value to students' work. Suggestion: When using checklists, rating scales, and rubrics, always provide the students with the assessment instrument *before* they begin working on the project or assignment.

The example of a rubric from this chapter corresponds to the concept map from a previous chapter. A quick review of the contents of that figure will be helpful. This is a sample of a student product that was completed over the course of several days. The central focus is the season of autumn. The students learned how insects, plants, animals, and trees change during autumn. Figure 16.2 shows the student work.

Appendix G is an example of a rubric or scoring rubric that will be designed to score the student work from chapter 16. Again, this was a student project that was completed over several days. The teacher could have created a grading instrument for every assignment. The concept map promotes long-term learning, learning?.

Specifications for this autumn assignment include the following:

- Create a concept map on the topic of autumn.
- Draw four categories for Level 1.
- Draw four categories for Level 2.
- The first level of the concept map will show insects, plants, trees, and animals.

- The second level of the concept map will show how each group relates to the first level.

The point distribution instantly shows the student the letter grade. (This was not tabulated in 10-point increments—90, 80, etc.) Because you distributed this information prior to the assignment and they had an opportunity to ask questions, you have taken every step to help the students to understand the criteria. Too often students wonder, "What does the teacher want me to do?" The answer to that is *learn*! But by making major efforts prior to the work time, the students know what is expected, it is in writing, and they can take it home to show their parents as well.

As with the checklist and rating scale, the rubric can be designed as a self-check, peer-graded, or teacher-graded assessment instrument. Appendix H shows the top portion of the same rubric that has been designed for multiple grading. Again, you can set this up in order to keep the identity of the peer anonymous.

- Summary for administrators: Many universities do not require a tests and measurements course for preservice teachers. This chapter would be a good resource for the new teachers at your school site who have not had that course. It gives a broad overview of test construction, administration, and also performance evaluations that would be helpful to new teachers. It also provides the reader with a huge set of examples and technology steps to construct those examples.

  I understand that part of your job is to check to be sure that teachers are recording student progress. This might be in the form of a checklist with younger students. The checklist information in this chapter will be helpful to these teachers when they design student portfolios.
- Summary for teachers: Perhaps you have wondered how to get those creative projects into a numerical grade form—and then be able to record them in the grade book. This chapter has taken you through the steps to complete that process.

- Summary for community volunteers and religious teachers: The beginning of this chapter offers a wealth of information for you. Your students will benefit from divergent questions that utilize higher order thinking skills and are at the top of Bloom's Taxonomy.
- Summary for parents: If you are a homeschool parent, this chapter has been a broad assessment overview for you. The point will come when you wonder if your child *knows* the information. The contents of this chapter will allow you to construct or create an evaluation instrument for you to assess learning.

APPENDIX A: CHECKLIST FOR KWL CHART DESIGNED FOR PEER, STUDENT, AND/OR TEACHER

KWL Chart—Penguins

☐ Student   ☐ Peer   ☐ Teacher

Completed on _____ Graded on _____

Student listed a minimum of one thing that he or she knew about penguins.	Yes	No
Student listed a minimum of two things that he or she wanted to know about penguins.	Yes	No
Student answered the first thing that he or she wanted to know.	Yes	No
Student answered the second thing that he or she wanted to know.	Yes	No

To create a checklist using Microsoft Word, go to Table, then Insert, then Table. Select the number of rows and columns. A row runs horizontally, like the rows of vegetables in your garden. Columns run vertically, like columns in architecture, such as the Parthenon. I adjusted the height of my rows to fit the content I wished to use.

To add the boxes that the individuals check, go to Insert, then Symbols. Select a box, and then select Insert and then Close.

APPENDIX B:
DESCRIPTIVE
RATING SCALE

Descriptive Rating Scale—Science

Student's name _____

Date _____

Due date for assignment _____

Circle the word that best describes the student's performance on this task.

A. The student put the slide into the microscope.

    Needs to improve   Acceptable   Target

B. The student focused the microscope.

    Needs to improve   Acceptable   Target

C. The student created a drawing of the slide and turned it in for grading.

    Needs to improve   Acceptable   Target

(continued)

Comments:

_____

_____

_____

_____

_____

_____

_____

_____

APPENDIX C:
GRAPHIC
RATING SCALE

Graphic Rating Scale—Science

Student's name _____

Date _____

Due date for assignment _____

Circle the symbol that best describes the student's performance on this task.

Needs to improve = ☐   Acceptable = △   Target = ○

A. The student put the slide into the microscope.

☐   △   ○

B. The student focused the microscope.

☐   △   ○

(continued)

C. The student created a drawing of the slide and turned it in for grading.

Comments:

_____

_____

_____

_____

Appendix C was created using Microsoft Word and following the steps in chapter 16.

To create the graphics on the graphic rating scale go to Insert, then Picture, then Autoshapes. You have a variety of choices from which to choose. You can manipulate the box around the shape to make it as large or small as you wish. You can also color the shape and print out the rating scale in color if you have that available to you.

APPENDIX D: NUMERICAL RATING SCALE

Numerical Rating Scale—Science

Student's name _____

Date _____

Due date for assignment _____

12 = Student work is at target level
 8 = Student work is acceptable
 4 = Student work needs to improve

A. The student put the slide into the microscope.

    12   8   4

B. The student focused the microscope.

    12   8   4

C. The student created a drawing of the slide and turned it in
   for grading.

    12   8   4

(continued)

Student's score _____

Total possible points = 36

Comments:

_____

_____

_____

_____

_____

APPENDIX E:
PEER-, SELF-, OR
TEACHER-GRADED
RATING SCALE

Numerical Rating Scale—Science
Student's name _____
Date _____
Due date for assignment _____
☐ Teacher   Date _____ Signature _____
☐ Student   Date _____ Signature _____
☐ Peer   Date _____ Signature _____

APPENDIX F:
GRAPHIC CHECKLIST

KWL Chart—Penguins		
☐ Student	☐ Peer	☐ Teacher

Completed on _____ Graded on _____

Circle the correct symbol to the right of each criterion.	Yes	No
Student listed a minimum of one thing that he/she knew about penguins.	◯	⊘
Student listed a minimum of two things that he/she wanted to know about penguins.	◯	⊘
Student answered the first thing that he/she wanted to know.	◯	⊘
Student answered the second thing that he/she wanted to know.	◯	⊘

APPENDIX G:
CONCEPT MAP

Concept Map—Autumn

Student's name _____

Date _____

Center
Create a concept map with the title of Autumn.
(5 points)

Concept Map
Show four categories for Level 1 and also for Level 2.
(24 points—3 points each)

Level 1
Four shapes containing the names of the areas studied.
(16 points—4 points each)

Level 2
Four shapes showing how Level 1 changes in autumn.
(16 points—4 points each)

(continued)

Total Point Value = 61 points

A = 61–55   B = 54–49   C = 48–43   D = 42–37   F = 36 & below

Comments:

_____

_____

_____

_____

APPENDIX H: RUBRIC DESIGNED FOR PEER, SELF, AND TEACHER SCORING

Concept Map—Autumn

Student's name _____

☐ Teacher   Date _____ Signature _____

☐ Student   Date _____ Signature _____

☐ Peer   Date _____ Signature _____

Center
Create a concept map with the title of Autumn
(5 points)

ABOUT THE AUTHOR

Dr. Linda Henshall Wilson is a professor at Northeastern State University in Oklahoma. She teaches elementary education courses to students majoring in elementary education, special education, and early childhood education, primarily elementary social studies methods and classroom management. Dr. Wilson makes frequent visits to schools in northeastern Oklahoma to work with first-year teachers. She is a three-time graduate of Oklahoma State University, with degrees in elementary education (BS), curriculum and instruction (MS), and educational leadership (EdD). Dr. Wilson holds numerous teaching certifications at the elementary and secondary levels as well as certifications as an elementary principal and superintendent of schools.

The fifth-generation Oklahoman taught students ranging from grades 1 through 12 for 18 1/2 years in public schools. She made the transition to higher education in 1998. Thus far, Dr. Wilson has taught 31 different higher education courses. Her experiences at the public school and higher education levels have given her a unique perspective into the realm of teaching and learning. These experiences have led to speaking opportunities at state, national, and international conferences on these topics. Dr. Wilson volunteers every semester with several schools to teach lessons and work with teachers on special learning projects for elementary students. She also volunteers at a local television station as the "education expert" each week, covering various educational topics for teachers, parents, and children.

Dr. Wilson is the author of *Teaching 201: Traveling Beyond the Basics* (ScarecrowEducation, 2001). This book focuses on the many aspects of teaching, while her second book targets learning in an enriched environment—long-term learning, learning[2]. Dr. Wilson may be contacted at teaching201@aol.com, www.nsuok.edu/, or www .drlindawilson.com.